© *[2025]* **Ethan Caldwell**

Disclaimer: The information contained in this book is for educational purposes only. While every effort has been made to ensure the accuracy of the content, the author and publisher disclaim any responsibility for errors or omissions. Readers are encouraged to seek professional advice where needed.

GO FOR WEB DEVELOPMENT

Build Scalable and Dynamic Web Applications with Ease.

By

Ethan Caldwell

Contents

Chapter 1: Introduction to Go and Web Development 7

1.1 Why Go for Web Development? 7
1.2 Setting Up Your Go Environment 14

1.3 Overview of Go's Features for Web Developers 23
1.4 Your First Web Server: "Hello, Web!" 33
Hands-On Exercise: Write and run a simple HTTP server that serves a static HTML page. 42
Chapter 2: Understanding HTTP and the net/http Package..52
2.1 Basics of HTTP and Its Role in Web Development 52

2.2 Anatomy of a Go HTTP Server 60

2.3 Handling Requests and Responses....................................72

2.4 Serving Static Files with Go..88

Hands-On Exercise: Build a server that serves CSS and image files along with HTML content. 98
Chapter 3: Routing and Middleware 107

....107
3.1 Introduction to Routing in Web Applications 107
3.2 Creating a Custom Router 117
3.3 Using Frameworks: Gin and Echo...................................129
3.4 Writing Middleware for Logging and Authentication......140
Hands-On Exercise: Create a basic router with custom routes and middleware for request logging. 154
Chapter 4: Templates and Dynamic Content 166

....166

4.1 Overview of the html/template Package 166

4.2 Rendering HTML Pages Dynamically 178

4.3 Handling Forms and User Input 191

4.4 Building a Simple Blog Template 204

Hands-On Exercise: Create a dynamic webpage that displays a list of blog posts fetched from a Go slice.................................215

Chapter 5: Building RESTful APIs 226

5.1 Principles of RESTful API Design......................226

5.2 Creating CRUD Endpoints in Go 234

5.3 Working with JSON Data 246

5.4 Testing APIs with Postman 260

Hands-On Project: Build a RESTful API for a task management application (e.g., To-Do List). 270

Chapter 6: Database Integration........................281

6.1 Introduction to SQL and NoSQL Databases 281

6.2 Connecting Go to a Database (PostgreSQL, MySQL) 287

6.3 Using GORM for Simplified Database Operations 297

6.4 Performing CRUD Operations........................308

Hands-On Project: Build a Go application that connects to a database to manage a list of products. 320

Chapter 7: Authentication and Authorization.....................333

7.1 Implementing User Authentication with JWT 333

7.2 OAuth Integration for Social Logins 347

7.3 Role-Based Access Control in Go 357

7.4 Securing Sensitive Endpoints...........................368

Hands-On Project: Add user authentication to the task management application built earlier.........................381

Chapter 8: Real-Time Web Applications with Websockets..395

8.1 Introduction to Websockets and Real-Time Features 395

8.2 Building a Real-Time Chat Application in Go.................405

8.3 Managing Concurrent Connections with Goroutines.....418

Hands-On Project: Develop a simple chat room application where multiple users can send and receive messages in real-time. 430

Chapter 9: Deployment and Scaling 444

9.1 Deploying Go Applications to Cloud Platforms (AWS, GCP, Heroku) 444

9.2 Containerization with Docker............................454

9.3 Scaling Web Applications with Load Balancers 464

9.4 Monitoring and Logging for Web Applications...............474

Hands-On Exercise: Deploy the task management application to a cloud platform using Docker. 487

Chapter 10: Complete Project: Building a Web Application 498

10.1 Project Overview: A Blog or E-Commerce Application .498

10.2 Setting Up the Backend with Go.......................504

10.3 Building RESTful APIs and Dynamic Templates 516

10.4 Adding Authentication and Real-Time Features 528

10.5 Deployment and Testing 542

Final Hands-On Project: Develop a complete, end-to-end web application and deploy it to production. 553

Appendices 569

Appendix A: Quick Reference for Go Syntax 569
Appendix B: Tools and Libraries for Web Development with Go
....582
Appendix C: Debugging and Troubleshooting Common Issues
....598

Chapter 1: Introduction to Go and Web Development

1.1 Why Go for Web Development?

When choosing a programming language for web development, the options can be overwhelming. However, Go (or Golang) stands out as a modern, efficient, and developer-friendly language that simplifies building robust web applications. Whether you're a beginner exploring web development or an experienced programmer seeking scalability, Go offers a compelling solution.

What Makes Go Unique?

Go was designed by engineers at Google to address real-world problems in software development, such as scalability, simplicity, and performance. Here's why Go is an excellent choice for web development:

Simplicity and Readability

Go's syntax is clean and concise, making it easy to learn and use. The language prioritizes simplicity, allowing developers to focus on solving problems rather than deciphering complex syntax. **Example:** Compare a simple "Hello, World!" HTTP server in Go with other

languages, and you'll see how straightforward Go is.
go

```go
package main

import (

  "fmt"

  "net/http"

)

func handler(w http.ResponseWriter, r *http.Request) {

  fmt.Fprintln(w, "Hello, World!")

}

func main() {

  http.HandleFunc("/", handler)

  http.ListenAndServe(":8080", nil)

}
```

1. **Explanation:**
   - The net/http package provides built-in support for web servers.
   - A single function (handler) handles incoming requests and sends responses.

2. **High Performance**

   Go is a compiled language, meaning it translates code directly into machine language. This makes it faster than interpreted languages like Python or JavaScript. Its performance is comparable to C and C++, making it ideal for resource-intensive web applications.
   Real-World Example:

   Companies like Uber and Netflix use Go to power their backend systems, which handle millions of requests per second.

Built-In Concurrency

Go's concurrency model, powered by Goroutines and Channels, allows you to efficiently manage multiple tasks simultaneously. This is crucial for web servers that need to handle thousands of concurrent connections.

Example:

Imagine a chat application where multiple users send messages simultaneously. Go's concurrency makes managing such interactions seamless.

go

```
package main
```

```go
import (

    "fmt"

    "time"

)

func printMessage(msg string) {

    for i := 0; i < 5; i++ {

        fmt.Println(msg)

        time.Sleep(1 * time.Second)

    }

}

func main() {

    go printMessage("Hello from Goroutine 1")

    go printMessage("Hello from Goroutine 2")

    time.Sleep(6 * time.Second) // Allow Goroutines to finish

}
```

3. **Explanation:**
    ○ go keyword starts a Goroutine (lightweight thread).

- Multiple Goroutines run concurrently, demonstrating Go's ability to handle parallel tasks.

---

4. **Scalability**

   Go's design makes it easy to scale applications. Its efficient memory management, garbage collection, and lightweight Goroutines enable developers to build systems that grow effortlessly with user demand.

   Case Study:

   Docker, the popular containerization platform, is written in Go. It handles billions of containers globally, showcasing Go's scalability.

Robust Standard Library

Go's standard library includes everything you need for web development, from HTTP servers to JSON parsing, without relying on third-party libraries.

Example:
Parsing JSON data is a common task in web development. Here's how simple it is in Go:

```go
package main

import (

    "encoding/json"

    "fmt"

)


type User struct {

    Name  string `json:"name"`

    Email string `json:"email"`

}


func main() {

    jsonData := `{"name": "Alice", "email": "alice@example.com"}`

    var user User

    json.Unmarshal([]byte(jsonData), &user)

    fmt.Printf("Name: %s, Email: %s\n", user.Name, user.Email)

}
```

5. **Explanation:**
   - The encoding/json package handles JSON parsing.
   - Struct tags (e.g., json:"name") map JSON fields to Go struct fields.

Hands-On Exercise: Exploring Go's Simplicity and Performance

Objective: Write a Go program to simulate handling multiple HTTP requests concurrently.

1. Create a file named concurrent_server.go.

Add the following code:
go

```
package main

import (

    "fmt"

    "net/http"

    "time"

)

func handler(w http.ResponseWriter, r *http.Request) {

    fmt.Fprintf(w, "Request received at: %s\n", time.Now().Format(time.RFC1123))
```

```go
}

func main() {

    http.HandleFunc("/", handler)

    fmt.Println("Server running on http://localhost:8080")

    http.ListenAndServe(":8080", nil)

}
```

2.

Run the server using:
go

```
go run concurrent_server.go
```

3. Open multiple browser tabs or use a tool like curl to send simultaneous requests to http://localhost:8080.

What You'll Learn:

- How Go handles multiple HTTP requests concurrently.
- The simplicity of Go's built-in HTTP server.

1.2 Setting Up Your Go Environment

Before diving into coding, it's essential to set up your Go development environment correctly. This chapter will guide you step-by-step to install Go, configure your workspace, and test your setup. By the end, you'll have a fully functional Go environment ready for web development.

Step 1: Installing Go

Go provides prebuilt installers for all major operating systems, making installation straightforward.

1. **Download Go**
    - Visit the official Go website: https://golang.org/dl/.
    - Select the installer for your operating system (Windows, macOS, or Linux).
2. **Run the Installer**
    - Follow the on-screen instructions to install Go.
    - The installer will set up the necessary files and add Go to your system's PATH.
3. **Verify Installation**
    - Open a terminal or command prompt.

Run the following command:
bash

```
go version
```

You should see output similar to:

go

```
go version go1.x.x <OS/Architecture>
```

   ○ This confirms Go is installed correctly.

Step 2: Setting Up Your Go Workspace

Go uses a workspace-based approach to organize your projects. Here's how to set it up:

1. **Create a Workspace Directory**
   ○ Choose a location for your Go projects. For example:
     ■ macOS/Linux: `~/go-projects`
     ■ Windows: `C:\go-projects`
2. **Understand Go's Directory Structure**
   ○ Go workspaces typically have three main directories:
     ■ `bin`: Contains compiled binaries.
     ■ `pkg`: Stores compiled package objects.
     ■ `src`: Contains your source code.
3. **Set the GOPATH Environment Variable**
   ○ The GOPATH variable tells Go where your workspace is located.
   ○ By default, Go uses `~/go` on macOS/Linux or `%USERPROFILE%\go` on Windows.
   ○ If you prefer a custom location, update your environment variables:

macOS/Linux: Add this line to your `.bashrc` or `.zshrc`:
bash

```
export GOPATH=~/go-projects

export PATH=$PATH:$GOPATH/bin
```

- Run `source ~/.bashrc` or `source ~/.zshrc` to apply changes.
- **Windows:**
  - Go to "System Properties" > "Environment Variables."
  - Add a new variable `GOPATH` with the value `C:\go-projects`.
  - Append `%GOPATH%\bin` to the `Path` variable.

4. **Test Your Workspace**

Create a new directory:
bash

```
mkdir -p $GOPATH/src/hello

cd $GOPATH/src/hello
```

Create a file named `main.go` with the following code:
go

```
package main
```

```go
import "fmt"

func main() {

    fmt.Println("Hello, Go Workspace!")

}
```

Run the program:
bash

```bash
go run main.go
```

You should see:

```
Hello, Go Workspace!
```

Step 3: Exploring Go Modules

Go modules are the standard for dependency management in modern Go projects.

1. **Initialize a Module**

Navigate to your project directory:
bash

```bash
cd $GOPATH/src/hello
```

Initialize a module:

bash

```
go mod init hello
```

- ○ This creates a go.mod file, which tracks your project's dependencies.

2. **Add Dependencies**

Let's add a third-party package, github.com/fatih/color, to enhance our program:

go

```
package main

import (

    "fmt"

    "github.com/fatih/color"

)

func main() {

    color.Cyan("Hello, Go Modules!")

    fmt.Println("This    is    a    colorful
message!")

}
```

Install the package:
bash

```
go mod tidy
```

Run the program:
bash

```
go run main.go
```

- ○ You should see a colorful "Hello, Go Modules!" message.

Step 4: Setting Up a Code Editor

While you can use any text editor, Visual Studio Code (VS Code) is highly recommended for Go development due to its excellent support and extensions.

1. **Install VS Code**
   - ○ Download and install VS Code from https://code.visualstudio.com/.
2. **Install the Go Extension**
   - ○ Open VS Code and go to the Extensions view (`Ctrl+Shift+X` or `Cmd+Shift+X` on macOS).
   - ○ Search for "Go" and install the official Go extension by the Go team.
3. **Configure VS Code for Go**
   - ○ Open your Go project in VS Code.

- The Go extension will prompt you to install additional tools. Click "Install All."
- Verify the setup by opening main.go and observing syntax highlighting and IntelliSense.

Hands-On Exercise: Build a Simple Go Program

Objective: Test your environment by writing a program that calculates the area of a rectangle.

Create a new project directory:
bash

```
mkdir -p $GOPATH/src/rectangle

cd $GOPATH/src/rectangle

go mod init rectangle
```

Write the program in main.go:
go

```
package main

import "fmt"

func main() {
```

```go
    length := 10.0

    width := 5.0

    area := length * width

    fmt.Printf("The area of the rectangle is: %.2f\n", area)

}
```

Run the program:
bash

```
go run main.go
```

You should see:
csharp

```
The area of the rectangle is: 50.00
```

What You'll Learn:

- How to set up and run a Go project.
- Basics of Go syntax and arithmetic operations.

1.3 Overview of Go's Features for Web Developers

Go (Golang) is a modern, efficient, and versatile programming language designed with simplicity and performance in mind. Its rich set of features makes it an excellent choice for web development, whether you're building small applications or large-scale systems. In this chapter, we'll explore Go's key features that empower web developers to build robust and scalable web applications.

1. Simplicity and Ease of Use

Go's clean syntax and minimalistic design make it easy to learn and use, even for beginners. It eliminates unnecessary complexity, allowing developers to focus on solving problems rather than dealing with intricate language constructs.

Example: A Simple HTTP Server

```go
package main

import (

    "fmt"

    "net/http"

)
```

```go
func    handler(w    http.ResponseWriter,    r
*http.Request) {

    fmt.Fprintln(w,    "Welcome    to    Go    Web
Development!")

}

func main() {

    http.HandleFunc("/", handler)

    http.ListenAndServe(":8080", nil)

}
```

Explanation:

- `http.HandleFunc` maps the root URL (`/`) to the `handler` function.
- `http.ListenAndServe` starts the server on port 8080.

Key Takeaway:
With just a few lines of code, you can set up a functional web server.

---

2. High Performance

Go is a compiled language, meaning it translates code directly into machine code. This results in faster execution compared to interpreted languages like Python or Ruby. Its performance is comparable to C or C++, making it suitable for high-performance web applications.

Real-World Use Case:

Netflix uses Go for its speed and efficiency in handling backend services, processing millions of requests per second.

---

3. Built-In Concurrency

Concurrency is crucial for web servers that handle multiple client requests simultaneously. Go's concurrency model, powered by Goroutines and Channels, is lightweight and easy to use.

Example: Handling Concurrent Requests

```go
package main

import (

    "fmt"

    "time"

)

func processRequest(id int) {

    fmt.Printf("Processing request %d\n", id)
```

```go
    time.Sleep(2 * time.Second) // Simulate a
time-consuming task

    fmt.Printf("Request %d processed\n", id)

}

func main() {

    for i := 1; i <= 5; i++ {

        go processRequest(i)

    }

    time.Sleep(5 * time.Second) // Allow
Goroutines to complete

}
```

Explanation:

- The `go` keyword starts a Goroutine, enabling concurrent execution.
- This example demonstrates handling multiple tasks simultaneously.

Key Takeaway:

Go's concurrency model is ideal for web applications that need to manage thousands of simultaneous connections.

4. Rich Standard Library

Go's standard library includes robust support for web development, eliminating the need for third-party dependencies in many cases.

Key Packages for Web Developers:

1. `net/http`: Build web servers and handle HTTP requests.
2. `encoding/json`: Parse and generate JSON data.
3. `html/template`: Render dynamic HTML templates.

Example: JSON Handling

```go
package main

import (

    "encoding/json"

    "fmt"

)

type User struct {

    Name  string `json:"name"`

    Email string `json:"email"`

}
```

```go
func main() {

    jsonData := `{"name": "Alice", "email": "alice@example.com"}`

    var user User

    json.Unmarshal([]byte(jsonData), &user)

    fmt.Printf("Name:  %s,  Email:  %s\n", user.Name, user.Email)

}
```

Explanation:

- The `encoding/json` package simplifies JSON parsing.
- Struct tags (e.g., `json:"name"`) map JSON fields to Go struct fields.

---

5. Scalability

Go's lightweight Goroutines, efficient memory management, and garbage collection make it highly scalable. Whether you're building a small blog or a distributed system, Go scales effortlessly.

Real-World Use Case:

Uber uses Go to power its real-time logistics platform, handling millions of rides and deliveries daily.

---

6. Strong Typing and Safety

Go's strong type system catches many errors at compile time, reducing runtime bugs. Its simplicity ensures developers write safe and predictable code.

Example: Type Safety

go

```go
package main

func addNumbers(a int, b int) int {

    return a + b

}

func main() {

    result := addNumbers(5, 10)

    println(result)

}
```

Key Takeaway:

Type safety ensures that operations are performed on compatible data types, minimizing errors.

---

7. Cross-Platform Support

Go compiles to a single binary executable, making deployment across different platforms straightforward. Its cross-platform capabilities are invaluable for web developers targeting diverse environments.

Example: Building for Multiple Platforms

bash

```
GOOS=linux GOARCH=amd64 go build -o app-linux

GOOS=windows GOARCH=amd64 go build -o app-windows.exe
```

Key Takeaway:

With simple commands, you can build applications for various operating systems.

Hands-On Exercise: Explore Go's Features

Objective: Build a simple web server that demonstrates Go's key features.

Create a new project directory:
bash

```
mkdir -p $GOPATH/src/feature-demo

cd $GOPATH/src/feature-demo

go mod init feature-demo
```

Write the program in `main.go`:
go

```
package main

import (

    "encoding/json"

    "fmt"

    "net/http"

)
```

```go
type Response struct {

    Message string `json:"message"`

}


func handler(w http.ResponseWriter, r
*http.Request) {

    response := Response{Message: "Hello, Go
Web Development!"}

    w.Header().Set("Content-Type",
"application/json")

    json.NewEncoder(w).Encode(response)

}


func main() {

    http.HandleFunc("/", handler)

    fmt.Println("Server running at
http://localhost:8080")

    http.ListenAndServe(":8080", nil)

}
```

Run the server:

bash

```
go run main.go
```

1. **Test the server:**
   - Open a browser and navigate to `http://localhost:8080`.

You should see a JSON response:

json

```
{"message":"Hello, Go Web Development!"}
```

1.4 Your First Web Server: "Hello, Web!"

Building your first web server in Go is a significant milestone. It's simple yet powerful, providing the foundation for more complex web applications. In this chapter, we'll create a basic HTTP server that responds with a friendly "Hello, Web!" message. By the end, you'll understand the key components of a Go web server and how to extend it for future projects.

Step 1: Understanding the net/http Package

The `net/http` package is the cornerstone of web development in Go. It provides everything needed to build and manage HTTP servers and clients. Key concepts include:

- **Handlers:** Functions that process HTTP requests and send responses.
- **ServeMux:** A multiplexer that routes requests to appropriate handlers.
- **ListenAndServe:** A function that starts the HTTP server.

Step 2: Writing Your First Web Server

Let's build a simple web server that responds with "Hello, Web!" to every request.

Create the Project Directory

Open your terminal and create a new directory for the project: bash

```
mkdir -p $GOPATH/src/hello-web

cd $GOPATH/src/hello-web

go mod init hello-web
```

Write the Code in `main.go`

Open your favorite code editor and create a file named `main.go` with the following content:

go

```
package main

import (

    "fmt"

    "net/http"

)

// handler function to process requests

func helloHandler(w http.ResponseWriter, r *http.Request) {

    fmt.Fprintln(w, "Hello, Web!")

}

func main() {

    // Map the root URL to the handler
function

    http.HandleFunc("/", helloHandler)
```

```go
    // Start the server on port 8080

    fmt.Println("Starting       server       at
http://localhost:8080")

    if  err  :=  http.ListenAndServe(":8080",
nil); err != nil {

        fmt.Println("Error           starting
server:", err)

    }

}
```

Run the Server

Save   the   file   and   run   the   server:
bash

```
go run main.go
```

You should see:
arduino

```
Starting server at http://localhost:8080
```

Test the Server

Open your browser and navigate to `http://localhost:8080`. You should see:

```
Hello, Web!
```

Step 3: How It Works

Let's break down the code:

1. **Importing Packages**
   - `fmt`: Used for formatted I/O operations.
   - `net/http`: Provides tools for HTTP communication.
2. **Handler Function**
   - `helloHandler`: A function that takes a `ResponseWriter` (to send responses) and a `Request` (to read client data).
   - `fmt.Fprintln(w, "Hello, Web!")`: Sends "Hello, Web!" as the HTTP response.
3. **Mapping Handlers**
   - `http.HandleFunc("/", helloHandler)`: Associates the root URL (`/`) with the `helloHandler` function.
4. **Starting the Server**
   - `http.ListenAndServe(":8080", nil)`: Starts the server on port 8080. The `nil` argument uses the default ServeMux for routing.

Step 4: Enhancing Your Web Server

Let's add more functionality to our server.

Example: Dynamic Greetings

Modify the `helloHandler` to respond with a personalized message based on a query parameter.

go

```go
func helloHandler(w http.ResponseWriter, r
*http.Request) {

    name := r.URL.Query().Get("name")

    if name == "" {

        name = "Web"

    }

    fmt.Fprintf(w, "Hello, %s!", name)

}
```

How It Works:

- `r.URL.Query().Get("name")`: Extracts the `name` query parameter from the URL.

38

- If `name` is not provided, it defaults to "Web."

Test It:

- Navigate to `http://localhost:8080?name=Alice`.

You should see:

```
Hello, Alice!
```

Step 5: Adding Error Handling

A good server gracefully handles errors. Let's add error handling to our server setup.

go

```go
func main() {
    fmt.Println("Starting        server        at
http://localhost:8080")

    err := http.ListenAndServe(":8080", nil)

    if err != nil {

        fmt.Println("Error            starting
server:", err)

    }
```

```
}
```

Key Takeaway:
This ensures that any issues during server startup are logged.

Hands-On Exercise: Build a Multi-Route Web Server

Objective: Extend your server to handle multiple routes.

Add More Handlers
Update main.go to include additional routes:
go

```go
func aboutHandler(w http.ResponseWriter, r
*http.Request) {

    fmt.Fprintln(w, "About Page: Welcome to
the Go Web Server!")

}

func contactHandler(w http.ResponseWriter, r
*http.Request) {

    fmt.Fprintln(w, "Contact Page: Email us
at contact@example.com")

}
```

```go
func main() {

    http.HandleFunc("/", helloHandler)

    http.HandleFunc("/about", aboutHandler)

    http.HandleFunc("/contact",
contactHandler)


    fmt.Println("Server        running        at
http://localhost:8080")

    if err := http.ListenAndServe(":8080",
nil); err != nil {

        fmt.Println("Error:", err)

    }

}
```

1. **Test the Routes**
   - Navigate to `http://localhost:8080/`: Displays "Hello, Web!"
   - Navigate to `http://localhost:8080/about`: Displays "About Page: Welcome to the Go Web Server!"
   - Navigate to `http://localhost:8080/contact`: Displays "Contact Page: Email us at contact@example.com."

Hands-On Exercise: Write and run a simple HTTP server that serves a static HTML page.

In this exercise, you'll build a simple HTTP server in Go that serves a static HTML page. This project is perfect for beginners to understand the fundamentals of serving web content, while also providing a solid foundation for more complex applications.

Objective

- Set up an HTTP server in Go.
- Serve a static HTML page to users.
- Understand how HTTP servers handle requests and serve responses.

Step 1: Understanding the Basics

Before diving into the code, let's understand the key concepts:

1. **HTTP**   **Server**

   An HTTP server listens for incoming client requests and responds with appropriate content, such as an HTML page.

2. **Static**   **HTML**

   Static HTML refers to web pages that do not change

dynamically. They are simple files stored on the server and served as-is to the client.

3. **Go's** `net/http` **Package**

   The `net/http` package provides tools to:

   ○ Start an HTTP server.

   ○ Handle client requests.

   ○ Serve files or dynamic content.

Step 2: Setting Up Your Project

Create a Project Directory

Open your terminal and create a new directory for the project:
bash

```
mkdir -p $GOPATH/src/static-server

cd $GOPATH/src/static-server

go mod init static-server
```

Prepare the HTML File

Inside the project directory, create a folder named `static` to store your HTML file:
bash

```
mkdir static
```

Create a file named `index.html` inside the `static` folder and add the following content:

html

```
<!DOCTYPE html>

<html lang="en">

<head>

    <meta charset="UTF-8">

    <meta                        name="viewport"
content="width=device-width,         initial-
scale=1.0">

    <title>Hello, Web!</title>

</head>

<body>

    <h1>Welcome   to   Your   First   Go   Web
Server</h1>

    <p>This is a static HTML page served by
your Go server.</p>

</body>

</html>
```

Step 3: Writing the Go Code

Create the Server Code

Create a file named main.go in the project directory and write the following code:

go

```go
package main

import (

    "fmt"

    "net/http"

)

func main() {

    // Serve static files from the "static"
directory

    fs                                    :=
http.FileServer(http.Dir("./static"))

    http.Handle("/", fs)


    // Start the server on port 8080
```

```go
    fmt.Println("Starting        server        at
http://localhost:8080")

    if  err  :=  http.ListenAndServe(":8080",
nil); err != nil {

        fmt.Println("Error                starting
server:", err)

    }

}
```

Step 4: How the Code Works

1. **Importing Packages**
   - `fmt`: For printing messages to the console.
   - `net/http`: To set up and manage the HTTP server.
2. **Serving Static Files**
   - `http.FileServer(http.Dir("./static")`
     `))`: Creates a file server that serves files from the `static` directory.
   - `http.Handle("/", fs)`: Maps the root URL (`/`) to the file server.
3. **Starting the Server**
   - `http.ListenAndServe(":8080", nil)`: Starts the server on port 8080, using the default request multiplexer (`nil`).

Step 5: Running the Server

Run the Server

Open your terminal and run the following command:
bash

```
go run main.go
```

You   should   see:
arduino

```
Starting server at http://localhost:8080
```

1. **Test the Server**

   Open your browser and navigate to
   `http://localhost:8080`. You should see the HTML
   page you created earlier, displaying:
   - A heading: "Welcome to Your First Go Web Server"
   - A paragraph: "This is a static HTML page served by your
     Go server."

Step 6: Enhancing the Server

1. Add Error Handling for Missing Files

Modify the file server to handle cases where a requested file does not
exist:

47

go

```go
http.HandleFunc("/",                    func(w
http.ResponseWriter, r *http.Request) {

    filePath := "./static" + r.URL.Path

    if          _,           err          :=
http.Dir("./static").Open(r.URL.Path);    err
!= nil {

        http.NotFound(w, r)

        return

    }

    http.ServeFile(w, r, filePath)

})
```

2. Add Logging for Requests

Log each incoming request to the console:

go

```go
http.HandleFunc("/",                    func(w
http.ResponseWriter, r *http.Request) {
```

```go
    fmt.Printf("Received request for: %s\n",
r.URL.Path)


http.FileServer(http.Dir("./static")).ServeH
TTP(w, r)

})
```

Step 7: Hands-On Exercise

Extend the HTML File

Add more content to index.html to make it visually appealing:
html

```html
<style>

    body {

        font-family: Arial, sans-serif;

        text-align: center;

        margin-top: 50px;

    }

</style>
```

Add More Static Files

Create an about.html file in the static directory:

html

```html
<!DOCTYPE html>

<html lang="en">

<head>

    <meta charset="UTF-8">

    <meta                        name="viewport"
content="width=device-width,        initial-
scale=1.0">

    <title>About</title>

</head>

<body>

    <h1>About This Server</h1>

    <p>This is a simple static file server
built with Go.</p>

</body>

</html>
```

1. **Test Navigation**
   Navigate to `http://localhost:8080/about.html`
   to view the new page.

Step 8: Deploying the Server

Build the Binary
Compile your server into an executable:
bash

```
go build -o static-server
```

1.

Run the Binary
Execute the binary:
bash

```
./static-server
```

2. **Deploy   on   a   Cloud   Server**
   Copy the binary and `static` folder to a cloud server and run
   it to serve your site online.

Chapter 2: Understanding HTTP and the net/http Package

The HTTP protocol is the backbone of the web, enabling communication between clients (browsers) and servers. In this chapter, we'll explore the basics of HTTP, dissect the anatomy of a Go HTTP server, and learn how to handle requests and responses. Finally, we'll build a hands-on project to serve static HTML, CSS, and image files using Go.

2.1 Basics of HTTP and Its Role in Web Development

The HyperText Transfer Protocol (HTTP) is the foundation of web communication, enabling clients (such as browsers) and servers to exchange information. In this section, we'll explore the fundamentals of HTTP, its components, and its importance in web development. By the end, you'll have a solid understanding of how HTTP works and why it's crucial for building web applications.

What is HTTP?

HTTP is a protocol that defines how messages are formatted and transmitted over the web. It operates on a request-response model:

- **Client**: Sends an HTTP request to the server.

- **Server**: Processes the request and sends back an HTTP response.

HTTP is stateless, meaning each request is independent, with no memory of previous interactions. This simplicity makes it lightweight and scalable, but additional mechanisms (like cookies or sessions) are needed for stateful interactions.

Core Components of HTTP

1. **Request**: The client initiates communication by sending a request to the server. A typical request consists of:
   - **Method**: Indicates the desired action (e.g., GET, POST).
   - **URL**: Specifies the resource being requested.
   - **Headers**: Provide metadata about the request (e.g., content type, user agent).
   - **Body**: Contains data sent to the server (e.g., form data).

Example:
vbnet

```
GET /index.html HTTP/1.1

Host: www.example.com
```

2. **Response**: The server replies with a response containing:
   - **Status Code**: Indicates the outcome of the request (e.g., 200 OK, 404 Not Found).

- **Headers**: Provide metadata about the response (e.g., content type, server name).
- **Body**: Contains the requested resource (e.g., HTML content).

Example:

less

```
HTTP/1.1 200 OK

Content-Type: text/html


<html><body>Hello, World!</body></html>
```

Common HTTP Methods

HTTP methods define the type of action the client wants to perform. The most common methods are:

Method	Description	Use Case
GET	Retrieve data	Fetching a webpage
POST	Send data to the server	Submitting a form

PUT	Update or replace a resource	Updating user information
DELETE	Remove a resource	Deleting a user account
HEAD	Retrieve headers only	Checking resource metadata

HTTP Status Codes

Status codes provide insight into the outcome of a request. They are grouped into five categories:

Code Range	Category	Example
1xx	Informational	101 Switching Protocols
2xx	Success	200 OK

3xx	Redirection	301 Moved Permanently
4xx	Client Error	404 Not Found
5xx	Server Error	500 Internal Server Error

The Role of HTTP in Web Development

HTTP is essential for web development because it:

- **Facilitates Communication**: It's the bridge between clients and servers.
- **Standardizes Interactions**: Ensures consistent data exchange across platforms.
- **Supports Modern Features**: HTTP/2 and HTTP/3 introduce faster, more secure communication.

Practical Example: Making an HTTP Request

Let's simulate an HTTP request and response using Go's `net/http` package.

Code Example: Simple HTTP Request

go

```go
package main

import (

    "fmt"

    "net/http"

)


func main() {

    // Make a GET request to a public API

    resp,                err                :=
http.Get("https://jsonplaceholder.typicode.c
om/posts/1")

    if err != nil {

        fmt.Println("Error:", err)

        return

    }

    defer resp.Body.Close()
```

```go
    // Print the status code

    fmt.Println("Status                Code:",
resp.StatusCode)


    // Print the response body

    body, err := io.ReadAll(resp.Body)

    if err != nil {

        fmt.Println("Error  reading  body:",
err)

        return

    }

    fmt.Println("Response                Body:",
string(body))

}
```

Explanation:

1. `http.Get`: Sends a GET request to the specified URL.
2. `resp.StatusCode`: Retrieves the HTTP status code from the response.
3. `io.ReadAll`: Reads the response body.

Hands-On Exercise: Exploring HTTP with cURL

cURL is a command-line tool for making HTTP requests. Let's use it to explore HTTP in action.

Step 1: Install cURL

Most systems come with cURL pre-installed. Verify by running:

bash

```
curl --version
```

Step 2: Make a GET Request

Fetch the homepage of a website:

bash

```
curl -v http://example.com
```

Output:

- **Request Line**: `GET / HTTP/1.1`
- **Response Headers**: Metadata like `Content-Type`.
- **Response Body**: The HTML content of the page.

Step 3: Experiment with Headers

Send a custom header:

bash

```
curl    -H    "User-Agent:    MyApp"
http://example.com
```

Step 4: Use Other Methods

Send a POST request with data:

bash

```
curl    -X    POST    -d    "name=John"
http://example.com/form
```

2.2 Anatomy of a Go HTTP Server

Building web applications in Go begins with understanding the structure of an HTTP server. The net/http package in Go provides powerful tools for creating web servers with minimal code. This chapter will break down the anatomy of a Go HTTP server, explaining each component step-by-step.

Core Components of a Go HTTP Server

A Go HTTP server typically consists of the following elements:

1. **HTTP Handlers**: Functions that process incoming requests and generate responses.
2. **Routing**: Mapping URLs to specific handlers.
3. **Server Initialization**: Configuring and starting the HTTP server.

Step-by-Step Guide to Building a Go HTTP Server

1. Import Required Packages

The `net/http` package is essential for building web servers. Additionally, `fmt` is commonly used for debugging and printing messages.

go

```
package main

import (

    "fmt"

    "net/http"

)
```

2. Create an HTTP Handler

An HTTP handler is a function that satisfies the `http.HandlerFunc` interface by implementing the `ServeHTTP` method. It processes requests and sends responses.

go

```go
func helloHandler(w http.ResponseWriter, r *http.Request) {

    fmt.Fprintln(w, "Hello, Web!")

}
```

- **Parameters**:
  - `w http.ResponseWriter`: Used to send responses back to the client.
  - `r *http.Request`: Contains information about the incoming request.
- **Example Response**: The `Fprintln` function writes "Hello, Web!" to the response writer.

3. Set Up Routing

Routing determines which handler function should be invoked for a given URL path. Use `http.HandleFunc` to associate a URL path with a handler.

go

```
func main() {

    http.HandleFunc("/", helloHandler)

}
```

- **Path** `/`: Matches the root URL of the server.
- **Handler**: `helloHandler` is invoked whenever the root URL is accessed.

---

4. Start the Server

The `http.ListenAndServe` function starts the HTTP server on a specified address and port.

go

```
func main() {

    http.HandleFunc("/", helloHandler)

    fmt.Println("Starting server on :8080")
```

63

```go
err := http.ListenAndServe(":8080", nil)

if err != nil {

    fmt.Println("Error                    starting
server:", err)

    }

}
```

- **Address :8080**: Indicates that the server will listen on port 8080.
- **Error Handling**: Logs any issues encountered while starting the server.

Complete Example: Basic HTTP Server

Here's the complete code for a simple Go HTTP server:

go

```go
package main

import (

    "fmt"

    "net/http"

)
```

```go
func helloHandler(w http.ResponseWriter, r
*http.Request) {

    fmt.Fprintln(w, "Hello, Web!")

}

func main() {

    http.HandleFunc("/", helloHandler)

    fmt.Println("Starting server on :8080")

    err := http.ListenAndServe(":8080", nil)

    if err != nil {

        fmt.Println("Error            starting
server:", err)

    }

}
```

Steps to Run the Server:

1. Save the code in a file named `main.go`.

Run the file using the command:
bash

```bash
go run main.go
```

2. Open a browser and navigate to `http://localhost:8080`. You should see "Hello, Web!" displayed.

Enhancing the Server

1. Adding More Routes

You can define additional handlers for different URL paths.

go

```go
func aboutHandler(w http.ResponseWriter, r *http.Request) {

    fmt.Fprintln(w, "About Page")

}

func main() {

    http.HandleFunc("/", helloHandler)

    http.HandleFunc("/about", aboutHandler)

    http.ListenAndServe(":8080", nil)

}
```

- **Path `/about`**: Invokes the `aboutHandler`.

2. Handling Query Parameters

Extract query parameters from the request URL.

go

```go
func queryHandler(w http.ResponseWriter, r
*http.Request) {

    query := r.URL.Query()

    name := query.Get("name")

    if name == "" {

        name = "Guest"

    }

    fmt.Fprintf(w, "Hello, %s!", name)

}


func main() {

    http.HandleFunc("/greet", queryHandler)

    http.ListenAndServe(":8080", nil)

}
```

- **Example URL**: `http://localhost:8080/greet?name=John`
- **Response**: "Hello, John!"

Real-World Applications

1. Serving JSON Responses

In modern web applications, JSON is a common data format. Use the `encoding/json` package to send JSON responses.

go

```go
import (

    "encoding/json"

    "net/http"

)

func  jsonHandler(w  http.ResponseWriter,  r
*http.Request) {

    data   :=   map[string]string{"message":
"Hello, Web!"}

    w.Header().Set("Content-Type",
"application/json")

    json.NewEncoder(w).Encode(data)
```

```go
}

func main() {

    http.HandleFunc("/json", jsonHandler)

    http.ListenAndServe(":8080", nil)

}
```

2. Handling Form Submissions

Parse form data from POST requests.

go

```go
func formHandler(w http.ResponseWriter, r *http.Request) {

    if r.Method == http.MethodPost {

        r.ParseForm()

        name := r.FormValue("name")

        fmt.Fprintf(w, "Form submitted by: %s", name)

    } else {

        http.Error(w, "Invalid request method", http.StatusMethodNotAllowed)
```

```go
    }
}

func main() {

    http.HandleFunc("/submit", formHandler)

    http.ListenAndServe(":8080", nil)

}
```

Practical Exercise: Multi-Route HTTP Server

Goal:

Build a server with the following routes:

1. `/`: Displays a welcome message.
2. `/about`: Provides information about the application.
3. `/json`: Returns a JSON response.

Code:

go

```go
package main

import (

    "encoding/json"
```

```go
    "fmt"

    "net/http"

)


func welcomeHandler(w http.ResponseWriter, r
*http.Request) {

    fmt.Fprintln(w, "Welcome to the Go HTTP
Server!")

}

func aboutHandler(w http.ResponseWriter, r
*http.Request) {

    fmt.Fprintln(w, "This is a simple HTTP
server built with Go.")

}

func jsonHandler(w http.ResponseWriter, r
*http.Request) {

    data := map[string]string{"status":
"success", "message": "Hello, JSON!"}

    w.Header().Set("Content-Type",
"application/json")
```

```go
        json.NewEncoder(w).Encode(data)

}


func main() {

    http.HandleFunc("/", welcomeHandler)

    http.HandleFunc("/about", aboutHandler)

    http.HandleFunc("/json", jsonHandler)

    fmt.Println("Server running on :8080")

    http.ListenAndServe(":8080", nil)

}
```

Steps:

1. Run the server.
2. Test each route in your browser or using `curl`.

2.3 Handling Requests and Responses

In web development, handling HTTP requests and responses is one of
the most fundamental tasks. The `net/http` package in Go makes it
simple to interact with the client, receive requests, and send
appropriate responses. This chapter will explore how to handle HTTP

requests and responses effectively, covering everything from basic request handling to parsing form data, managing headers, and returning dynamic content.

Understanding HTTP Requests

An HTTP request consists of several parts:

- **Method**: Specifies the type of operation (e.g., GET, POST).
- **Headers**: Provide metadata about the request (e.g., content type, user agent).
- **Body**: Contains the data sent by the client (in POST requests).
- **URL**: Identifies the resource being requested.

In Go, the `http.Request` object encapsulates all of this information, making it easy to interact with.

Handling GET Requests

The most common HTTP method is GET. It retrieves data from the server. Go's `http.Request` object provides several ways to access the details of a GET request.

Example: Handling a Simple GET Request

go

```go
package main

import (

    "fmt"

    "net/http"

)

func getHandler(w http.ResponseWriter, r *http.Request) {

    // r.Method gives us the HTTP method used (GET, POST, etc.)

    if r.Method == http.MethodGet {

        // Respond with a simple message

        fmt.Fprintln(w, "This is a GET request!")

    } else {

        http.Error(w, "Invalid request method", http.StatusMethodNotAllowed)

    }
```

```
}

func main() {

    http.HandleFunc("/", getHandler)

    http.ListenAndServe(":8080", nil)

}
```

- `r.Method`: Checks if the request method is GET.
- `fmt.Fprintln(w, "This is a GET request!")`: Sends a simple message back to the client.

Running the Example

1. Run the server using `go run main.go`.
2. Open a browser and go to `http://localhost:8080/`.
3. You should see the message: "This is a GET request!"

Handling POST Requests

POST requests are used to send data to the server, typically from forms or APIs. The data is usually included in the request body.

Example: Handling a POST Request

go

```go
package main

import (

    "fmt"

    "net/http"

)

func postHandler(w http.ResponseWriter, r
*http.Request) {

    if r.Method == http.MethodPost {

        // Parse form data

        r.ParseForm()

        // Extract form values

        name := r.FormValue("name")

        age := r.FormValue("age")


        // Respond with the received data
```

```go
        fmt.Fprintf(w, "Received data: Name
= %s, Age = %s", name, age)

    } else {

        http.Error(w,    "Invalid    request
method", http.StatusMethodNotAllowed)

    }

}

func main() {

    http.HandleFunc("/", postHandler)

    http.ListenAndServe(":8080", nil)

}
```

- **r.ParseForm()**: Parses the form data from the request body.
- **r.FormValue("name")**: Retrieves the value of the form field named "name".

Testing the POST Handler

1. Run the server.

Use curl or a tool like Postman to send a POST request:
bash

```
curl    -X    POST    -d    "name=John&age=30"
http://localhost:8080/
```

The server should respond with:

kotlin
```
Received data: Name = John, Age = 30
```

Handling Query Parameters

Query parameters are often used in GET requests to pass data to the server. These parameters are included in the URL after the ? symbol.

Example: Handling Query Parameters

go

```
package main

import (

    "fmt"

    "net/http"

)

func queryHandler(w http.ResponseWriter, r
*http.Request) {
```

```go
    // Extract query parameters using
r.URL.Query()

    query := r.URL.Query()

    name := query.Get("name")

    age := query.Get("age")


    // Provide a response based on query
parameters

    if name != "" && age != "" {

        fmt.Fprintf(w, "Hello %s, you are %s
years old.", name, age)

    } else {

        http.Error(w,      "Missing      query
parameters", http.StatusBadRequest)

    }

}


func main() {

    http.HandleFunc("/", queryHandler)
```

```
    http.ListenAndServe(":8080", nil)

}
```

- **r.URL.Query()**: Retrieves all the query parameters as a `map[string][]string`.
- **query.Get("name")**: Extracts the value of the `name` parameter.

Testing the Query Parameters Handler

1. Run the server.

Open a browser and visit:
ruby

```
http://localhost:8080/?name=Alice&age=25
```

2. You should see the message: "Hello Alice, you are 25 years old."

Working with Headers

HTTP headers provide additional information about the request or the response. Common headers include `Content-Type`, `User-Agent`, and `Authorization`.

Example: Reading and Setting Headers

go

```go
package main

import (

    "fmt"

    "net/http"

)

func headerHandler(w http.ResponseWriter, r
*http.Request) {

    // Read a custom header

    userAgent := r.Header.Get("User-Agent")


    // Set a response header

    w.Header().Set("X-Custom-Header",
"GoServer")


    // Respond with the User-Agent

    fmt.Fprintf(w, "Your User-Agent: %s",
userAgent)

}
```

```go
func main() {

    http.HandleFunc("/", headerHandler)

    http.ListenAndServe(":8080", nil)

}
```

- `r.Header.Get("User-Agent")`: Reads the User-Agent header from the request.
- `w.Header().Set("X-Custom-Header", "GoServer")`: Sets a custom response header.

Testing the Header Handler

1. Run the server.

Use `curl` to send a request with a custom header:
bash

```bash
curl -H "User-Agent: MyCustomAgent" http://localhost:8080/
```

The server should respond with:
sql

```sql
Your User-Agent: MyCustomAgent
```

Sending JSON Responses

In modern web applications, it's common to send and receive JSON data. Go makes it easy to work with JSON using the `encoding/json` package.

Example: Sending JSON Responses

go

```
package main

import (

    "encoding/json"

    "fmt"

    "net/http"

)

func jsonHandler(w http.ResponseWriter, r
*http.Request) {

    // Data to send in the response

    data := map[string]string{"message":
"Hello, Web!"}
```

```go
    // Set the Content-Type to
application/json

    w.Header().Set("Content-Type",
"application/json")


    // Encode and send the JSON response

    json.NewEncoder(w).Encode(data)

}


func main() {

    http.HandleFunc("/", jsonHandler)

    http.ListenAndServe(":8080", nil)

}
```

- `json.NewEncoder(w).Encode(data)`: Converts the data map to JSON and sends it as a response.

Testing the JSON Handler

1. Run the server.

Use `curl` to send a GET request:

bash

```
curl http://localhost:8080/
```

The server should respond with:

json

```
{"message":"Hello, Web!"}
```

Practical Exercise: Build a Form Handler

Goal:

Create a web server that:

1. Displays a form where the user can input their name and age.
2. Submits the form via POST and displays a personalized message.

Steps:

1. Create an HTML form.
2. Handle the form submission in Go.

go

```
package main

import (
```

```go
    "fmt"

    "net/http"

)

func formHandler(w http.ResponseWriter, r
*http.Request) {

    if r.Method == http.MethodPost {

        r.ParseForm()

        name := r.FormValue("name")

        age := r.FormValue("age")

        fmt.Fprintf(w, "Hello %s, you are %s
years old.", name, age)

    } else {

        // Display the form

        fmt.Fprintln(w, `

            <form method="POST">

                Name: <input type="text"
name="name"><br>

                Age: <input type="text"
name="age"><br>
```

```
                <input        type="submit"
value="Submit">

            </form>

        `)

    }

}


func main() {

    http.HandleFunc("/", formHandler)

    http.ListenAndServe(":8080", nil)

}
```

Steps:

1. Run the server.
2. Open a browser and visit `http://localhost:8080/`.
3. Fill out the form and submit it. The server should respond with a personalized message.

2.4 Serving Static Files with Go

In web development, serving static files—such as HTML, CSS, JavaScript, and image files—is a fundamental task. Go makes this process incredibly simple with the built-in `http.ServeFile` function and the `http.FileServer` handler. In this chapter, we will explore how to serve static files using Go, including how to organize your project, handle requests for static assets, and efficiently serve them to clients.

What Are Static Files?

Static files are files that do not change dynamically on the server. They are served as-is, meaning the server just reads the file and sends it directly to the client. Examples of static files include:

- **HTML files**: Used for the structure of web pages.
- **CSS files**: Used to style HTML elements.
- **JavaScript files**: Used to add interactivity to web pages.
- **Image files**: Such as `.jpg`, `.png`, `.gif`, etc.

These files are typically stored in a directory on the server and can be accessed by the client through URLs.

Serving Static Files with http.ServeFile

The http.ServeFile function is a simple way to serve individual static files. It takes two arguments:

- w: The http.ResponseWriter that is used to send the file to the client.
- r: The http.Request that contains information about the request, such as the file path.

Example: Serving a Single Static File

Let's start by serving a simple HTML file using http.ServeFile.

1. **Create a directory for your project** (e.g., go-static-example).
2. **Inside the directory, create an HTML file** called index.html with the following content:

html

```
<!DOCTYPE html>

<html lang="en">

<head>

    <meta charset="UTF-8">

    <meta                      name="viewport"
content="width=device-width,       initial-
scale=1.0">
```

```
<title>Static File Example</title>

</head>

<body>

    <h1>Welcome    to    the    Static    File
Example!</h1>

    <p>This is a static HTML page served by
Go.</p>

</body>

</html>
```

3. **Create a Go file** (e.g., main.go) with the following code to serve the HTML file:

go

```
package main

import (

    "net/http"

    "fmt"

)
```

```go
func serveHTML(w http.ResponseWriter, r
*http.Request) {

    // Serve the HTML file located at the
specified path

    http.ServeFile(w, r, "index.html")

}


func main() {

    http.HandleFunc("/", serveHTML)

    fmt.Println("Server is running on
http://localhost:8080")

    http.ListenAndServe(":8080", nil)

}
```

- **http.ServeFile(w, r, "index.html")**: This serves the index.html file when the root URL (/) is requested.
- **http.HandleFunc("/", serveHTML)**: This tells the server to call serveHTML whenever the root URL is requested.

Running the Example

1. Open a terminal and navigate to the project directory.

Run the server with:
bash

```
go run main.go
```

2. Open a web browser and go to `http://localhost:8080/`.
3. You should see the HTML content displayed in the browser.

Serving Static Files from a Directory

In real-world applications, you often need to serve multiple static files like CSS, JavaScript, and image files. Instead of serving each file individually, Go provides an easy way to serve all files from a specific directory using `http.FileServer`.

Example: Serving Static Files from a Directory

Let's modify the project to serve all static files (HTML, CSS, and images) from a directory.

1. **Create a directory named `static`** inside your project folder.
2. **Move your `index.html` file into the `static` directory**.
3. **Create a CSS file** called `style.css` inside the `static` directory with the following content:

css

```css
body {

    font-family: Arial, sans-serif;

    background-color: #f4f4f9;

    text-align: center;

}

h1 {

    color: #333;

}
```

4. **Modify the `main.go` file** to serve the entire static directory:

go

```go
package main

import (

    "net/http"

    "fmt"

)

func main() {
```

```
    // Serve all files in the 'static'
directory
    http.Handle("/static/",
http.StripPrefix("/static/",
http.FileServer(http.Dir("static"))))


    fmt.Println("Server    is    running    on
http://localhost:8080")

    http.ListenAndServe(":8080", nil)

}
```

- **http.StripPrefix("/static/",**
  http.FileServer(http.Dir("static"))): This
  line tells the server to serve files from the static directory
  when a request is made to the /static/ URL path.
    - http.FileServer(http.Dir("static")):
      This serves the files in the static directory.
    - http.StripPrefix("/static/",   ...):
      This removes the /static/ part from the URL path
      before looking for the file in the directory.

Testing the Static File Server

Run the server again:

bash

```
go run main.go
```

1. Open a browser and go to:
   - http://localhost:8080/static/index.html to view the HTML page.
   - http://localhost:8080/static/style.css to view the CSS file.

Serving Images and Other Static Assets

Serving images and other media files works the same way as serving HTML and CSS files. Let's add an image to the static directory.

1. **Download or create an image** and save it as image.jpg inside the static directory.
2. **Modify the index.html file** to reference the image:

html

```
<!DOCTYPE html>

<html lang="en">

<head>
```

```html
    <meta charset="UTF-8">

    <meta                    name="viewport"
content="width=device-width,         initial-
scale=1.0">

    <title>Static File Example</title>

    <link                   rel="stylesheet"
href="/static/style.css">

</head>

<body>

    <h1>Welcome    to    the    Static    File
Example!</h1>

    <p>This is a static HTML page served by
Go.</p>

    <img              src="/static/image.jpg"
alt="Example Image">

</body>

</html>
```

- `<img src="/static/image.jpg" alt="Example Image">`: This references the image from the `static` directory.

Testing the Static Assets

1. Run the server.
2. Visit `http://localhost:8080/static/index.html` in your browser.
3. You should see the HTML page with the CSS styling and the image.

Best Practices for Serving Static Files

When serving static files in Go, here are a few best practices to keep in mind:

- **Use `http.ServeFile` for single files**: For small applications where you only need to serve a few files, `http.ServeFile` is simple and effective.
- **Use `http.FileServer` for directories**: When serving multiple files (like CSS, JS, and images), `http.FileServer` is the best choice. It's efficient and reduces the need to manually handle each file.
- **Set proper cache headers**: To improve performance, consider setting caching headers for static files. This allows browsers to

cache the files locally, reducing the need to re-download them for each request.

- **Serve compressed files**: Consider serving compressed versions of your static files (like `.gzip` or `.brotli`), especially for large files like images and JavaScript, to improve load times.

Hands-On Exercise: Build a server that serves CSS and image files along with HTML content.

In this hands-on exercise, we will build a Go web server that serves a combination of HTML, CSS, and image files. This project will help you understand how to structure a Go server that handles multiple types of static content and serves them efficiently.

We will go step by step, covering everything from setting up the project to running the server and verifying the output in the browser.

Project Overview

We will create a simple Go server that serves:

- An **HTML file** that displays a basic webpage.
- A **CSS file** to style the webpage.
- An **image** to display on the webpage.

The server will handle requests for these files and serve them correctly to the client.

Step 1: Set Up Your Project Directory

Create a project directory: Create a folder on your computer where you will store the Go code and static files. For example, name it go-static-server.

bash

```
mkdir go-static-server

cd go-static-server
```

Create subdirectories for static content: Inside the project directory, create a subdirectory named static where you will store the HTML, CSS, and image files.

bash

```
mkdir static
```

Create the HTML file: Inside the static directory, create a file named index.html. This file will be the main webpage.

html

```html
<!-- static/index.html -->

<!DOCTYPE html>

<html lang="en">
```

```html
<head>

    <meta charset="UTF-8">

    <meta                     name="viewport"
content="width=device-width,        initial-
scale=1.0">

    <title>My Static Website</title>

    <link                  rel="stylesheet"
href="/static/style.css">

</head>

<body>

    <h1>Welcome to My Static Website</h1>

    <p>This is a simple Go web server serving
static files.</p>

    <img    src="/static/image.jpg"    alt="A
beautiful landscape">

</body>

</html>
```

Create the CSS file: Inside the static directory, create a file named style.css. This file will style the HTML content. css

100

```css
/* static/style.css */
body {
    font-family: Arial, sans-serif;
    background-color: #f4f4f9;
    text-align: center;
}

h1 {
    color: #333;
}

img {
    max-width: 100%;
    height: auto;
    border-radius: 8px;
}
```

1.

2. **Add an image**: Inside the static directory, add an image file named image.jpg. You can use any image file you like for this project. If you don't have one, download a free image from a website like Unsplash or Pexels.

Step 2: Create the Go Web Server

Now, let's create the Go server that will serve these static files.

Create the main Go file: In the root directory (go-static-server), create a Go file named main.go. This file will contain the code to start the web server. go

```go
package main

import (

    "fmt"

    "net/http"

)

func main() {

    // Serve static files from the 'static'
directory
```

```go
    http.Handle("/static/",
http.StripPrefix("/static/",
http.FileServer(http.Dir("static"))))


    // Handle the root URL and serve the HTML
file

    http.HandleFunc("/",                func(w
http.ResponseWriter, r *http.Request) {

        // Serve the HTML file located in the
'static' directory

        http.ServeFile(w,                    r,
"static/index.html")

    })


    // Start the server on port 8080

    fmt.Println("Server    is    running    on
http://localhost:8080")

    if err := http.ListenAndServe(":8080",
nil); err != nil {

        fmt.Println("Error            starting
server:", err)
```

```
        }

}
```

1. **Explanation of the Code:**
   - ```
     http.Handle("/static/",
     http.StripPrefix("/static/",
     http.FileServer(http.Dir("static"))
     )):
     ```
     - This line sets up the server to serve static files from the static directory. When a request is made to the /static/ URL path, Go will serve the corresponding file from the static folder.
     - `http.StripPrefix("/static/", ...)` ensures that the /static/ part of the URL is removed before looking for the file in the static directory.
   - ```
     http.HandleFunc("/",             func(w
     http.ResponseWriter,               r
     *http.Request) {...}):
     ```
     - This sets up a handler for the root URL (/). When a request is made to the root URL, the server will serve the index.html file from the static directory.
   - ```
     http.ListenAndServe(":8080", nil):
     ```
     - This starts the server on port 8080. If there is an error starting the server, it will be printed to the console.
     ```

Step 3: Run the Server

1. Open a terminal and navigate to the project directory (`go-static-server`).

Run the Go server using the following command:
bash

```
go run main.go
```

2. You should see the message `Server is running on http://localhost:8080` in the terminal.

Step 4: Test the Server in Your Browser

1. Open a web browser and go to `http://localhost:8080`.
2. You should see the webpage displayed with the following elements:
   - The title **"My Static Website"** in the browser tab.
   - The heading **"Welcome to My Static Website"** on the page.
   - The image you added in the `static` directory should be displayed below the text.

3. If you inspect the page (right-click and select "Inspect" or press `Ctrl+Shift+I`), you will see that the CSS file is applied to the page, and the image is loaded correctly.

Step 5: Troubleshooting

If you run into any issues, here are some common problems and their solutions:

1. **404 Error for Static Files**:
   - Ensure that the files are in the correct `static` directory.
   - Check that the file paths in the HTML are correct (e.g., `/static/style.css` for the CSS file).
2. **Server Not Running**:
   - Make sure you ran `go run main.go` in the correct directory.
   - If you see an error starting the server, double-check the code for typos or missing imports.
3. **Images Not Displaying**:
   - Ensure the image file is in the `static` directory and that the file name in the HTML matches the actual image file name (e.g., `image.jpg`).

Chapter 3: Routing and Middleware

Routing and middleware are essential components of any web application. They define how incoming requests are handled and allow you to modify the behavior of your application dynamically. In this chapter, we will explore routing concepts, create custom routes, and introduce middleware for tasks like logging and authentication.

3.1 Introduction to Routing in Web Applications

Routing is the backbone of any web application. It determines how incoming requests are directed to specific parts of your application, enabling users to interact with different functionalities. In Go, routing is straightforward, thanks to its robust `net/http` package and the availability of third-party frameworks like Gin and Echo.

This chapter introduces the fundamentals of routing in web applications, explores how it works in Go, and provides practical examples to solidify your understanding.

What Is Routing?

Routing is the process of mapping a URL or endpoint to a specific function or handler in your application. It's like a GPS system for your web server, ensuring that each request reaches its intended destination.

For example:

- **URL**: `http://example.com/home`
- **Handler**: A function that generates and sends the "Home Page" content to the user.

Why Is Routing Important?

Routing enables:

1. **Organization**: Keeps your application modular and maintainable by mapping specific tasks to specific routes.
2. **User Experience**: Allows users to navigate seamlessly through different sections of your application.
3. **Dynamic Behavior**: Handles user-specific requests like fetching a profile or processing a form.

Routing in Go

Go's standard `net/http` package includes basic routing capabilities. It allows you to define routes and their corresponding handlers using the `http.HandleFunc` function.

Basic Example

go

```
package main

import (
```

```go
    "fmt"

    "net/http"
)


func homeHandler(w http.ResponseWriter, r *http.Request) {

    fmt.Fprintln(w, "Welcome to the Home Page!")

}


func aboutHandler(w http.ResponseWriter, r *http.Request) {

    fmt.Fprintln(w, "This is the About Page.")

}


func main() {

    http.HandleFunc("/", homeHandler) // Root route
```

```
    http.HandleFunc("/about", aboutHandler)
// About route


    fmt.Println("Server    is    running    at
http://localhost:8080")

    http.ListenAndServe(":8080", nil)

}
```

Explanation

1. **Handlers:** Functions like homeHandler and
   aboutHandler process requests and send responses.
2. **http.HandleFunc**: Maps a URL path (e.g., /about) to
   a specific handler.
3. **http.ListenAndServe**: Starts the server and listens on a
   specified port (8080 in this case).

How Routing Works in Go

When a user visits a URL:

1. The Go server receives the request.
2. The router determines the handler associated with the
   requested path.

3. The handler processes the request and sends a response.

Dynamic Routing

Static routes like /about are useful but limited. Dynamic routes allow you to handle paths with variable components, such as /user/123.

Example: Parsing Dynamic Paths

```go
package main

import (

    "fmt"

    "net/http"

    "strings"

)

func userHandler(w http.ResponseWriter, r *http.Request) {

    path := strings.TrimPrefix(r.URL.Path, "/user/")

    fmt.Fprintf(w, "Hello, User %s!", path)
```

```
}

func main() {

    http.HandleFunc("/user/", userHandler)


    fmt.Println("Server     is     running     at
http://localhost:8080")

    http.ListenAndServe(":8080", nil)

}
```

How It Works

- **Dynamic Segment**: The `strings.TrimPrefix` function
  extracts the dynamic part of the URL (e.g., `123` from
  `/user/123`).
- **Response**: The handler personalizes the response based on the
  dynamic segment.

Advanced Routing with Third-Party Frameworks

Go's `net/http` package is sufficient for simple applications, but
third-party frameworks like Gin and Echo simplify routing for larger
projects.

Example: Using Gin for Routing

go

```go
package main

import (

    "github.com/gin-gonic/gin"

)

func main() {

    router := gin.Default()


    router.GET("/", func(c *gin.Context) {

        c.String(200, "Welcome to the Home
Page!")

    })


    router.GET("/user/:id",            func(c
*gin.Context) {

        id := c.Param("id")

        c.String(200, "Hello, User %s!", id)
```

```
    })


    router.Run(":8080")
}
```

Benefits of Using Frameworks

1. **Simplified Syntax**: Cleaner and more intuitive routing.
2. **Features**: Built-in support for middleware, JSON handling, and more.
3. **Scalability**: Better suited for complex applications.

Hands-On Exercise: Creating a Basic Router

Objective

Build a simple Go server with routes for a homepage and a user profile page.

Steps

1. **Create a new project**:
   - Open your terminal and create a directory: `mkdir basic-router`.
   - Navigate to the directory: `cd basic-router`.
2. **Write the code**:

```go
package main

import (

    "fmt"

    "net/http"

)

func homeHandler(w http.ResponseWriter, r
*http.Request) {

    fmt.Fprintln(w, "Welcome to the Home
Page!")

}


func profileHandler(w http.ResponseWriter, r
*http.Request) {

    fmt.Fprintln(w, "This is the User Profile
Page.")

}


func main() {
```

```go
    http.HandleFunc("/", homeHandler)

    http.HandleFunc("/profile",
profileHandler)


    fmt.Println("Server        running        at
http://localhost:8080")

    http.ListenAndServe(":8080", nil)

}
```

3. **Run the server**:
   - Execute `go run main.go` in your terminal.
4. **Test the application**:
   - Open a browser and visit:
     - `http://localhost:8080` for the homepage.
     - `http://localhost:8080/profile` for the profile page.

Expected Output

- Visiting / displays: **"Welcome to the Home Page!"**
- Visiting `/profile` displays: **"This is the User Profile Page."**

3.2 Creating a Custom Router

In web development, a router directs incoming requests to the appropriate handler functions based on the URL and HTTP method. While Go's `net/http` package provides basic routing capabilities, building a custom router can offer greater flexibility and control over your application's behavior.

In this chapter, we'll explore how to create a custom router from scratch. By the end, you'll understand how routing works under the hood and how to implement features like dynamic routing and method-specific handling.

Why Create a Custom Router?

A custom router is useful when:

1. **You Need Flexibility**: Implement features tailored to your application's specific requirements.
2. **Learning Purposes**: Understand how routing works at a deeper level.
3. **Performance Optimization**: Create lightweight solutions for specific use cases.

Designing a Custom Router

A basic router should:

1. **Map Routes to Handlers**: Store URL patterns and their corresponding handler functions.
2. **Support HTTP Methods**: Distinguish between GET, POST, etc.
3. **Handle Dynamic Routes**: Process paths with variables like `/user/:id`.

Step 1: Define the Router Structure

We'll start by defining a `Router` struct to hold route information.

go

```go
package main

import (

    "fmt"

    "net/http"

    "strings"

)
```

```go
// Route struct to hold path and handler
type Route struct {
    Path    string

    Method  string

    Handler http.HandlerFunc
}


// Router struct to manage routes
type Router struct {
    Routes []Route
}
```

Explanation

- **Route:** Represents a single route with a path, HTTP method, and handler function.
- **Router:** Holds a slice of routes for managing multiple endpoints.

Step 2: Add a Method to Register Routes

We'll add a `Handle` method to register routes in the `Router`.

go

```go
// Handle method to add a route
func (r *Router) Handle(method, path string,
handler http.HandlerFunc) {

    r.Routes = append(r.Routes, Route{Path:
path, Method: method, Handler: handler})

}
```

How It Works

- **Method**: Specifies the HTTP method (e.g., GET, POST).
- **Path**: Defines the route's URL pattern.
- **Handler**: Associates the route with a function to handle requests.

Step 3: Implement the ServeHTTP Method

The `ServeHTTP` method will match incoming requests to the appropriate route and call the corresponding handler.

go

```go
// ServeHTTP method to process requests
func (r *Router) ServeHTTP(w http.ResponseWriter, req *http.Request) {
    for _, route := range r.Routes {
        if route.Path == req.URL.Path && route.Method == req.Method {
            route.Handler(w, req)
            return
        }
    }
    http.NotFound(w, req) // Handle unmatched routes
}
```

How It Works

1. **Loop Through Routes**: Checks each route for a matching path and method.

2. **Call Handler**: Invokes the handler if a match is found.

3. **Fallback**: Returns a 404 error for unmatched routes.

Step 4: Add Dynamic Route Support

To support dynamic routes like /user/:id, we'll modify the matching logic.

go

```
// Match dynamic routes

func (r *Router) matchDynamicRoute(routePath, requestPath string) bool {

    routeParts := strings.Split(routePath, "/")

    requestParts := strings.Split(requestPath, "/")


    if len(routeParts) != len(requestParts) {

        return false

    }
```

```go
    for i, part := range routeParts {

        if    part   !=   requestParts[i]   &&
!strings.HasPrefix(part, ":") {

            return false

        }

    }

    return true

}
```

Explanation

- **Route Parts:** Splits the route and request paths into segments.
- **Dynamic Matching**: Allows segments starting with : to match any value.

Modify ServeHTTP to use this logic:

go

```go
func    (r    *Router)    ServeHTTP(w
http.ResponseWriter, req *http.Request) {

    for _, route := range r.Routes {
```

```go
        if   r.matchDynamicRoute(route.Path,
req.URL.Path) && route.Method == req.Method {

            route.Handler(w, req)

            return

        }

    }

    http.NotFound(w, req)

}
```

Step 5: Build a Complete Example

Here's a complete example of a custom router in action.

go

```go
package main

import (

    "fmt"

    "net/http"

    "strings"

)
```

```go
type Route struct {

    Path    string

    Method  string

    Handler http.HandlerFunc

}


type Router struct {

    Routes []Route

}



func (r *Router) Handle(method, path string,
handler http.HandlerFunc) {

    r.Routes = append(r.Routes, Route{Path:
path, Method: method, Handler: handler})

}



func (r *Router) matchDynamicRoute(routePath,
requestPath string) bool {
```

```go
    routeParts := strings.Split(routePath,
"/")

    requestParts                        :=
strings.Split(requestPath, "/")


    if len(routeParts) != len(requestParts) {

        return false

    }


    for i, part := range routeParts {

        if part != requestParts[i] &&
!strings.HasPrefix(part, ":") {

            return false

        }

    }

    return true

}
```

```go
func        (r        *Router)        ServeHTTP(w
http.ResponseWriter, req *http.Request) {

    for _, route := range r.Routes {

        if    r.matchDynamicRoute(route.Path,
req.URL.Path) && route.Method == req.Method {

            route.Handler(w, req)

            return

        }

    }

    http.NotFound(w, req)

}


func main() {

    router := &Router{}


    router.Handle("GET",        "/",        func(w
http.ResponseWriter, r *http.Request) {

        fmt.Fprintln(w, "Welcome to the Home
Page!")
```

```go
    })


    router.Handle("GET", "/user/:id", func(w
http.ResponseWriter, r *http.Request) {

        parts := strings.Split(r.URL.Path,
"/")

        userID := parts[len(parts)-1]

        fmt.Fprintf(w, "Hello, User %s!",
userID)

    })


    fmt.Println("Server is running at
http://localhost:8080")

    http.ListenAndServe(":8080", router)

}
```

Testing the Custom Router

Run the server:

bash

```
go run main.go
```

1. Test the routes:

   o Visit `http://localhost:8080/` → Displays
      "Welcome to the Home Page!".

   o Visit `http://localhost:8080/user/123` →
      Displays **"Hello, User 123!"**.

3.3 Using Frameworks: Gin and Echo

Frameworks simplify web development by providing pre-built tools and abstractions that reduce boilerplate code. In this chapter, we'll explore two popular Go frameworks: **Gin** and **Echo**. These frameworks streamline routing, middleware, and request handling, enabling developers to build robust web applications quickly.

By the end of this chapter, you'll understand the core features of both frameworks and how to use them effectively in your projects.

Why Use a Framework?

While Go's `net/http` package is powerful and lightweight, frameworks like Gin and Echo offer:

1. **Simplified Syntax**: Cleaner and more concise code for routing and middleware.
2. **Performance**: Optimized for speed and scalability.
3. **Extensibility**: Built-in support for common tasks like JSON handling, request validation, and more.
4. **Community Support**: Rich ecosystems with plugins, documentation, and examples.

Getting Started with Gin

Gin is a fast, lightweight framework designed for building high-performance web applications.

Installing Gin

To install Gin, run the following command:

bash

```
go get -u github.com/gin-gonic/gin
```

Basic Usage

Here's how to create a simple Gin application:

go

```go
package main

import (

    "github.com/gin-gonic/gin"

)

func main() {

    // Create a new Gin router

    router := gin.Default()


    // Define a GET route

    router.GET("/", func(c *gin.Context) {

        c.JSON(200, gin.H{

            "message": "Welcome to Gin!",

        })

    })
```

```go
// Start the server

router.Run(":8080")
}
```

Explanation

1. **gin.Default()**: Creates a router with default middleware (logging and recovery).
2. **router.GET()**: Defines a route for HTTP GET requests.
3. **c.JSON()**: Sends a JSON response to the client.

Adding Parameters

Gin supports dynamic routes with parameters.

go

```go
router.GET("/user/:id", func(c *gin.Context) {
    id := c.Param("id")
    c.JSON(200, gin.H{
        "user_id": id,
    })
```

```
})
```

Access the route /user/123 to see:
json

```json
{

  "user_id": "123"

}
```

Middleware in Gin

Middleware in Gin allows you to process requests before they reach the handler.

go

```go
func Logger() gin.HandlerFunc {

    return func(c *gin.Context) {

        // Log request details

        c.Next()

    }

}
```

```go
func main() {

    router := gin.Default()

    router.Use(Logger())

    router.GET("/", func(c *gin.Context) {

        c.JSON(200, gin.H{"message": "Hello,
World!"})

    })

    router.Run(":8080")

}
```

Getting Started with Echo

Echo is another popular framework known for its simplicity and performance.

Installing Echo

To install Echo, run:

bash

```bash
go get -u github.com/labstack/echo/v4
```

Basic Usage

Here's how to create a simple Echo application:

go

```go
package main

import (

    "net/http"

    "github.com/labstack/echo/v4"

)

func main() {

    // Create a new Echo instance

    e := echo.New()


    // Define a GET route

    e.GET("/", func(c echo.Context) error {

        return          c.JSON(http.StatusOK,
map[string]string{
```

```go
        "message": "Welcome to Echo!",
      })
   })


   // Start the server

   e.Start(":8080")

}
```

Explanation

1. **echo.New()**: Creates a new Echo instance.
2. **e.GET()**: Defines a route for HTTP GET requests.
3. **c.JSON()**: Sends a JSON response to the client.

Adding Parameters

Echo supports route parameters like Gin:

go

```go
e.GET("/user/:id", func(c echo.Context) error
{
    id := c.Param("id")
```

```go
        return                c.JSON(http.StatusOK,
map[string]string{

        "user_id": id,

    })

})
```

Middleware in Echo

Middleware in Echo is easy to define and use.

go

```go
func       Logger(next        echo.HandlerFunc)
echo.HandlerFunc {

    return func(c echo.Context) error {

        // Log request details

        return next(c)

    }

}

func main() {
```

```
e := echo.New()

e.Use(Logger)

e.GET("/", func(c echo.Context) error {
    return      c.JSON(http.StatusOK,
map[string]string{"message":      "Hello,
World!"})
```

Feature	Gin	Echo
Performance	High	High
Syntax	Concise and flexible	Minimal and intuitive
Middleware	Simple to implement	Simple to implement
Community	Large and active	Large and active
Built-in Features	JSON, routing, middleware	JSON, routing, middleware

```go
    })

    e.Start(":8080")

}
```

Comparing Gin and Echo

Hands-On Example: A CRUD API with Gin and Echo

Gin Example

go

```go
router.GET("/items", getAllItems)

router.POST("/items", createItem)

router.PUT("/items/:id", updateItem)

router.DELETE("/items/:id", deleteItem)
```

Echo Example

go

```go
e.GET("/items", getAllItems)
```

```
e.POST("/items", createItem)

e.PUT("/items/:id", updateItem)

e.DELETE("/items/:id", deleteItem)
```

3.4 Writing Middleware for Logging and Authentication

Middleware is a powerful concept in web development that allows you to intercept and process requests before they reach the final handler. In Go, middleware is commonly used for tasks like logging, authentication, request validation, and more. This chapter will guide you through creating middleware for logging and authentication, two essential components of any web application.

What Is Middleware?

Middleware acts as a bridge between the client request and the server's response. It's like a pipeline where you can inspect, modify, or reject requests before they are passed to the handler.

Common Use Cases for Middleware

1. **Logging**: Record request details for debugging or analytics.
2. **Authentication**: Verify user credentials before granting access.

3. **Authorization**: Ensure the user has the right permissions.
4. **Rate Limiting**: Prevent abuse by limiting the number of requests.
5. **Error Handling**: Standardize error responses across your application.

Middleware in Go's `net/http`

In Go, middleware is typically implemented as a function that wraps an `http.Handler`.

Basic Middleware Structure

go

```go
func Middleware(next http.Handler)
http.Handler {

    return http.HandlerFunc(func(w
http.ResponseWriter, r *http.Request) {

        // Pre-processing logic

        next.ServeHTTP(w, r)

        // Post-processing logic

    })

}
```

Creating a Logging Middleware

Logging middleware records details about incoming requests, such as the HTTP method, URL, and response time.

Code Example

go

```go
package main

import (

    "log"

    "net/http"

    "time"

)

func LoggingMiddleware(next http.Handler)
http.Handler {

    return              http.HandlerFunc(func(w
http.ResponseWriter, r *http.Request) {

        start := time.Now()

        log.Printf("Started %s %s", r.Method,
r.URL.Path)
```

```go
        next.ServeHTTP(w, r)


        duration := time.Since(start)

        log.Printf("Completed  %s  in  %v",
r.URL.Path, duration)

    })

}


func main() {

    mux := http.NewServeMux()

    mux.HandleFunc("/",                 func(w
http.ResponseWriter, r *http.Request) {

        w.Write([]byte("Hello,
Middleware!"))

    })


    loggedMux := LoggingMiddleware(mux)
```

```go
    http.ListenAndServe(":8080", loggedMux)
}
```

Explanation

1. `start := time.Now()`: Records the start time of the request.
2. `log.Printf()`: Logs the HTTP method and URL.
3. `next.ServeHTTP()`: Calls the next handler in the chain.
4. `time.Since(start)`: Calculates the duration of the request.

Creating Authentication Middleware

Authentication middleware ensures that only authenticated users can access certain endpoints.

Code Example

go

```go
package main

import (

    "net/http"

)
```

```go
func    AuthMiddleware(next    http.Handler)
http.Handler {

    return              http.HandlerFunc(func(w
http.ResponseWriter, r *http.Request) {

        token                           :=
r.Header.Get("Authorization")

        if token != "valid-token" {

            http.Error(w,    "Unauthorized",
http.StatusUnauthorized)

            return

        }


        next.ServeHTTP(w, r)

    })

}


func main() {

    mux := http.NewServeMux()
```

```go
    mux.HandleFunc("/secure",            func(w
http.ResponseWriter, r *http.Request) {

        w.Write([]byte("Welcome to the secure
endpoint!"))

    })


    secureMux := AuthMiddleware(mux)


    http.ListenAndServe(":8080", secureMux)

}
```

Explanation

1. `r.Header.Get("Authorization")`: Retrieves the token from the `Authorization` header.
2. `http.Error()`: Sends a 401 Unauthorized response if the token is invalid.
3. `next.ServeHTTP()`: Proceeds to the next handler if the token is valid.

Middleware in Gin

Gin simplifies middleware implementation with its `gin.HandlerFunc`.

Logging Middleware in Gin

go

```go
package main

import (

    "log"

    "time"


    "github.com/gin-gonic/gin"

)


func LoggingMiddleware() gin.HandlerFunc {

    return func(c *gin.Context) {

        start := time.Now()

        log.Printf("Started    %s    %s",
c.Request.Method, c.Request.URL.Path)
```

```go
        c.Next()


        duration := time.Since(start)

        log.Printf("Completed  %s  in  %v",
c.Request.URL.Path, duration)

    }

}


func main() {

    r := gin.Default()

    r.Use(LoggingMiddleware())


    r.GET("/", func(c *gin.Context) {

        c.JSON(200, gin.H{"message": "Hello,
Middleware!"})

    })
```

```go
    r.Run(":8080")

}
```

Authentication Middleware in Gin

go

```go
func AuthMiddleware() gin.HandlerFunc {

    return func(c *gin.Context) {

        token                                    :=
c.GetHeader("Authorization")

        if token != "valid-token" {

            c.AbortWithStatusJSON(401,
gin.H{"error": "Unauthorized"})

            return

        }


        c.Next()

    }

}
```

```go
func main() {

    r := gin.Default()

    r.Use(AuthMiddleware())


    r.GET("/secure", func(c *gin.Context) {

        c.JSON(200,          gin.H{"message":
"Welcome to the secure endpoint!"})

    })


    r.Run(":8080")

}
```

Middleware in Echo

Echo also provides a simple way to implement middleware.

Logging Middleware in Echo

go

```go
package main

import (

    "github.com/labstack/echo/v4"

    "time"

)

func                     LoggingMiddleware(next
echo.HandlerFunc) echo.HandlerFunc {

    return func(c echo.Context) error {

        start := time.Now()

        c.Logger().Infof("Started   %s   %s",
c.Request().Method, c.Request().URL.Path)


        err := next(c)


        duration := time.Since(start)

        c.Logger().Infof("Completed   %s   in
%v", c.Request().URL.Path, duration)

        return err
```

```go
        }
}


func main() {

    e := echo.New()

    e.Use(LoggingMiddleware)


    e.GET("/", func(c echo.Context) error {
        return                      c.JSON(200,
map[string]string{"message":         "Hello,
Middleware!"})

    })


    e.Start(":8080")
}
```

Authentication Middleware in Echo

go

```go
func  AuthMiddleware(next  echo.HandlerFunc)
echo.HandlerFunc {
```

```go
    return func(c echo.Context) error {

        token :=
c.Request().Header.Get("Authorization")

        if token != "valid-token" {

            return c.JSON(401,
map[string]string{"error": "Unauthorized"})

        }

        return next(c)

    }

}


func main() {

    e := echo.New()

    e.Use(AuthMiddleware)


    e.GET("/secure", func(c echo.Context)
error {
```

```
        return                    c.JSON(200,
map[string]string{"message": "Welcome to the
secure endpoint!"})

    })


    e.Start(":8080")

}
```

Hands-On Exercise: Create a basic router with custom routes and middleware for request logging.

In this hands-on exercise, we will build a basic web server in Go that uses custom routes and middleware to log incoming requests. This project is designed to solidify your understanding of routing and middleware while giving you practical experience with Go's net/http package.

What You'll Learn

1. How to set up a basic router with custom routes.
2. How to implement middleware for request logging.
3. How to combine routing and middleware to build a functional web server.

Step 1: Setting Up the Project

Prerequisites

Ensure you have the following installed on your system:

- Go (version 1.19 or higher)
- A text editor or IDE (e.g., VS Code, GoLand)

Create the Project Directory

1. Open your terminal.

Create a new directory for your project:
bash

```
mkdir go-router-middleware

cd go-router-middleware
```

Initialize a Go module:
bash

```
go mod init go-router-middleware
```

Step 2: Writing the Code

Create the Main File

Create a new file named `main.go` in your project directory.

Code Overview

We will:

1. Set up a router with custom routes.
2. Implement middleware for logging.
3. Combine the router and middleware in the `main` function.

Step 3: Implementing the Router

Start by creating a router with custom routes.

go

```go
package main

import (

    "fmt"

    "net/http"

)

// HomeHandler handles requests to the home
route.
```

```go
func HomeHandler(w http.ResponseWriter, r
*http.Request) {

    fmt.Fprintln(w, "Welcome to the Home
Page!")

}



// AboutHandler handles requests to the about
route.

func AboutHandler(w http.ResponseWriter, r
*http.Request) {

    fmt.Fprintln(w, "This is the About
Page.")

}



// ContactHandler handles requests to the
contact route.

func ContactHandler(w http.ResponseWriter, r
*http.Request) {

    fmt.Fprintln(w, "Contact us at
contact@example.com.")
```

```
}
```

Step 4: Adding Middleware for Request Logging

Middleware will log the HTTP method and URL of each incoming request.

go

```
// LoggingMiddleware logs the details of
incoming requests.

func LoggingMiddleware(next http.Handler)
http.Handler {

    return              http.HandlerFunc(func(w
http.ResponseWriter, r *http.Request) {

        fmt.Printf("Received %s request for
%s\n", r.Method, r.URL.Path)

        next.ServeHTTP(w, r) // Call the
next handler

    })

}
```

Step 5: Combining the Router and Middleware

Set up the router, wrap it with middleware, and start the server.

go

```go
func main() {

    // Create a new ServeMux (router)

    mux := http.NewServeMux()


    // Register routes

    mux.HandleFunc("/", HomeHandler)

    mux.HandleFunc("/about", AboutHandler)

    mux.HandleFunc("/contact",
ContactHandler)


    // Wrap  the  router  with  the  logging
middleware

    loggedRouter := LoggingMiddleware(mux)


    // Start the server
```

```go
    fmt.Println("Server    is    running    on
http://localhost:8080")

    http.ListenAndServe(":8080",
loggedRouter)

}
```

Step 6: Running the Server

1. Open your terminal and navigate to the project directory.

Run the server:
bash

```bash
go run main.go
```

2. Open your browser and test the following routes:
    o http://localhost:8080/
    o http://localhost:8080/about
    o http://localhost:8080/contact

Each request will be logged in the terminal.

Step 7: Testing and Enhancing

Expected Output in the Terminal

When you visit `http://localhost:8080/about`, the terminal should display:

bash

```
Received GET request for /about
```

Enhancements

1. **Add More Routes**: Expand the router to include additional endpoints.
2. **Extend Middleware**: Log more details, such as headers or query parameters.

Complete Code

Here's the complete `main.go` file:

go

```go
package main

import (

    "fmt"

    "net/http"
```

```
)


// HomeHandler handles requests to the home
route.

func HomeHandler(w http.ResponseWriter, r
*http.Request) {

    fmt.Fprintln(w, "Welcome to the Home
Page!")

}


// AboutHandler handles requests to the about
route.

func AboutHandler(w http.ResponseWriter, r
*http.Request) {

    fmt.Fprintln(w, "This is the About
Page.")

}

// ContactHandler handles requests to the
contact route.
```

```go
func ContactHandler(w http.ResponseWriter, r
*http.Request) {

    fmt.Fprintln(w,      "Contact      us      at
contact@example.com.")

}

// LoggingMiddleware logs the details of
incoming requests.

func   LoggingMiddleware(next   http.Handler)
http.Handler {

    return              http.HandlerFunc(func(w
http.ResponseWriter, r *http.Request) {

        fmt.Printf("Received %s request for
%s\n", r.Method,
```

go

```go
        r.URL.Path)

        next.ServeHTTP(w,  r)  //  Call  the
next handler

    })

}
```

```go
func main() {

    // Create a new ServeMux (router)

    mux := http.NewServeMux()


    // Register routes

    mux.HandleFunc("/", HomeHandler)

    mux.HandleFunc("/about", AboutHandler)

    mux.HandleFunc("/contact",
ContactHandler)


    // Wrap the router with the logging
middleware

    loggedRouter := LoggingMiddleware(mux)


    // Start the server

    fmt.Println("Server is running on
http://localhost:8080")
```

```
    http.ListenAndServe(":8080",
loggedRouter)

}
```

Understanding the Code

1. **Router**: The `http.NewServeMux()` creates a multiplexer that directs incoming requests to the appropriate handler.
2. **Handlers**: Each route (e.g., `/about`) is linked to a specific function that generates a response.
3. **Middleware**: The `LoggingMiddleware` wraps the router, intercepting requests to log their details before passing them to the appropriate handler.
4. **Server**: The `http.ListenAndServe` function starts the HTTP server, listening on port `8080`.

Real-World Applications

1. **Custom Routes**: Use this pattern to create APIs for applications, such as `/api/users` or `/api/products`.
2. **Middleware**: Add authentication, error handling, or rate limiting to secure and optimize your application.

Chapter 4: Templates and Dynamic Content

Dynamic content is at the heart of modern web applications. In this chapter, we'll explore how to use Go's `html/template` package to create dynamic, data-driven web pages. You'll learn to handle user input, render HTML templates, and build a simple blog template.

4.1 Overview of the html/template Package

html/template Package

The html/template package is a cornerstone of web development in Go, offering powerful tools to generate dynamic HTML content securely and efficiently. In this section, we'll explore its key features, syntax, and best practices to help you build robust web applications.

What is the `html/template` Package?

The `html/template` package is part of Go's standard library, designed specifically for rendering HTML templates. It ensures that any user-provided data is properly escaped, protecting your application from cross-site scripting (XSS) attacks.

Why Use `html/template`?

- **Dynamic Content Generation**: Easily embed dynamic data into HTML.
- **Security**: Automatically escapes potentially malicious input.
- **Flexibility**: Supports conditional logic, loops, and template inheritance.
- **Efficiency**: Integrates seamlessly with Go's `net/http` package.

Core Concepts

Templates and Data Binding

Templates are files or strings containing placeholders for dynamic data. The `html/template` package replaces these placeholders with actual values when rendering the template.

Template Syntax

- **Data Insertion**: Use `{{ . }}` to insert data.
- **Control Flow**:
  - `{{ if }}` for conditionals.
  - `{{ range }}` for iterating over slices or arrays.
- **Template Functions**: Built-in functions like `len`, `print`, and more enhance flexibility.

Setting Up a Basic Template

Step 1: Create a Template File

1. Create a folder named `templates` in your project directory.
2. Inside `templates`, create a file named `base.html` with the following content:

html

```
<!DOCTYPE html>

<html lang="en">

<head>

    <meta charset="UTF-8">

    <meta                         name="viewport"
content="width=device-width,           initial-
scale=1.0">

    <title>{{.Title}}</title>

</head>

<body>

    <h1>{{.Heading}}</h1>

    <p>{{.Content}}</p>

</body>
```

```
</html>
```

Step 2: Write Go Code to Render the Template

Here's how you can load and render the base.html template in Go:

go

```go
package main

import (

    "html/template"

    "net/http"

)


// PageData holds the dynamic data for the
template

type PageData struct {

    Title    string

    Heading string

    Content string

}
```

```go
func HomeHandler(w http.ResponseWriter, r *http.Request) {

    // Parse the template file

    tmpl, err := template.ParseFiles("templates/base.html")

    if err != nil {

        http.Error(w, "Error loading template", http.StatusInternalServerError)

        return

    }

    // Data to pass to the template

    data := PageData{

        Title:   "Welcome to Go Templates",

        Heading: "Hello, World!",

        Content: "This page is dynamically generated using the html/template package.",

    }


    // Render the template
```

```go
    err = tmpl.Execute(w, data)

    if err != nil {

        http.Error(w,    "Error    rendering
template", http.StatusInternalServerError)

    }

}


func main() {

    http.HandleFunc("/", HomeHandler)

    http.ListenAndServe(":8080", nil)

}
```

Step 3: Run the Application

Start the server:

bash

```
go run main.go
```

1. Open your browser and navigate to
   `http://localhost:8080`. You should see the rendered
   HTML page.

Understanding Template Syntax

Data Insertion

- Use `{{ . }}` to access the root data object.
- Use `{{ .FieldName }}` to access specific fields in a struct.

Example:

html

```
<h1>{{.Title}}</h1>

<p>{{.Content}}</p>
```

Control Flow

- **Conditionals:**

html

```
{{ if .IsAdmin }}

    <p>Welcome, Admin!</p>

{{ else }}

    <p>Welcome, User!</p>

{{ end }}
```

- **Loops**:

html

```
<ul>

    {{ range .Items }}

        <li>{{ . }}</li>

    {{ end }}

</ul>
```

Template Functions

Go provides several built-in functions:

- `len`: Returns the length of a collection.
- `print`: Prints values.
- `html`: Escapes raw HTML.

Example:

html

```
<p>Total items: {{ len .Items }}</p>
```

Best Practices

1. **Organize Templates**: Use a dedicated folder for templates to keep your project organized.
2. **Separate Logic and Presentation**: Avoid embedding business logic in templates. Keep templates focused on presentation.
3. **Use Template Caching**: Parse templates once during application startup to improve performance.

Example:

go

```go
var tmpl = template.Must(template.ParseFiles("templates/base.html"))


func HomeHandler(w http.ResponseWriter, r *http.Request) {

    data := PageData{

        Title:   "Cached Template Example",

        Heading: "Using Template Caching",

        Content: "This template is parsed only once during startup.",
```

```go
    }

    tmpl.Execute(w, data)

}
```

Hands-On Exercise

Objective

Create a webpage that displays a list of items dynamically using the `html/template` package.

Steps

1. Create a new template file, `list.html`:

html

```html
<!DOCTYPE html>

<html lang="en">

<head>

    <meta charset="UTF-8">

    <meta                         name="viewport"
content="width=device-width,        initial-
scale=1.0">
```

175

```html
    <title>Dynamic List</title>
</head>
<body>
    <h1>Items</h1>
    <ul>
        {{ range . }}
            <li>{{ . }}</li>
        {{ end }}
    </ul>
</body>
</html>
```

2. Add a handler in `main.go`:

go

```go
func ListHandler(w http.ResponseWriter, r *http.Request) {
    tmpl, err := template.ParseFiles("templates/list.html")
```

```go
    if err != nil {

        http.Error(w,    "Error    loading
template", http.StatusInternalServerError)

        return

    }



    items := []string{"Item 1", "Item 2",
"Item 3", "Item 4"}

    tmpl.Execute(w, items)

}
```

3. Update the `main` function:

go

```go
func main() {

    http.HandleFunc("/", HomeHandler)

    http.HandleFunc("/list", ListHandler)

    http.ListenAndServe(":8080", nil)

}
```

4. Visit `http://localhost:8080/list` to see the dynamic list.

4.2 Rendering HTML Pages Dynamically

Dynamic rendering is at the heart of web development. It enables web applications to adapt their content based on user input, database queries, or other variables. In this chapter, we'll explore how to render HTML pages dynamically using Go's `html/template` package, with clear examples and practical exercises.

What Does "Rendering Dynamically" Mean?

Dynamic rendering involves creating HTML pages on the fly, embedding data into predefined templates. Instead of serving static HTML files, dynamic rendering tailors content to user needs, making applications more interactive and personalized.

For example, consider a web page displaying a list of products. With dynamic rendering, the list can change based on the user's preferences or search criteria.

Key Steps in Dynamic Rendering

1. **Define a Template**: Create an HTML file with placeholders for dynamic data.
2. **Parse the Template**: Load and prepare the template for rendering.
3. **Bind Data to the Template**: Pass a data structure to populate the placeholders.
4. **Render the Template**: Send the generated HTML to the user's browser.

Step-by-Step Guide

Step 1: Create a Template File

Start by creating a folder named `templates`. Inside it, create a file called `product.html` with the following content:

html

```
<!DOCTYPE html>

<html lang="en">

<head>

    <meta charset="UTF-8">
```

```
    <meta                         name="viewport"
content="width=device-width,              initial-
scale=1.0">

    <title>{{.Title}}</title>

</head>

<body>

    <h1>{{.Heading}}</h1>

    <ul>

        {{ range .Products }}

            <li>{{ . }}</li>

        {{ end }}

    </ul>

</body>

</html>
```

This template includes placeholders for a title, heading, and a list of products.

Step 2: Define a Data Structure

180

In Go, you need a struct to hold the data you want to render dynamically.

go

```go
type PageData struct {
    Title    string

    Heading  string

    Products []string
}
```

This struct defines fields corresponding to the placeholders in the template.

Step 3: Write the Go Code

Here's the code to render the `product.html` template dynamically:

go

```go
package main

import (

    "html/template"

    "net/http"
```

```go
)

// PageData holds the dynamic data for the
template

type PageData struct {

    Title    string

    Heading  string

    Products []string

}

func ProductHandler(w http.ResponseWriter, r
*http.Request) {

    // Parse the template file

    tmpl,            err            :=
template.ParseFiles("templates/product.html"
)

    if err != nil {

        http.Error(w,    "Error    loading
template", http.StatusInternalServerError)

        return

    }
```

```go
    // Data to pass to the template

    data := PageData{

        Title:    "Product List",

        Heading: "Our Products",

        Products:         []string{"Laptop",
"Smartphone", "Tablet", "Smartwatch"},

    }

    // Render the template

    err = tmpl.Execute(w, data)

    if err != nil {

        http.Error(w,    "Error    rendering
template", http.StatusInternalServerError)

    }

}

func main() {

    http.HandleFunc("/products",
ProductHandler)

    http.ListenAndServe(":8080", nil)

}
```

Detailed Explanation of the Code

Template Parsing:

The `template.ParseFiles` function reads the template file and prepares it for rendering.

go

```go
tmpl, err :=
template.ParseFiles("templates/product.html"
)
```

Data Binding:

The `PageData` struct holds the data, and an instance of it is created with sample values:

go

```go
data := PageData{

    Title:    "Product List",

    Heading:  "Our Products",

    Products:              []string{"Laptop",
"Smartphone", "Tablet", "Smartwatch"},

}
```

Rendering the Template:

The `Execute` method replaces the placeholders in the template with the actual data and writes the result to the HTTP response. go

```go
err = tmpl.Execute(w, data)
```

1. **Error Handling**:
   Errors during parsing or rendering are handled gracefully by returning an appropriate HTTP status code.

Testing the Application

Run the application:
bash

```bash
go run main.go
```

1. Open your browser and visit `http://localhost:8080/products`.

You should see a dynamically generated page listing the products.

Adding More Complexity

Conditional Rendering

You can conditionally display content based on data values.

html

```
{{ if .Products }}

    <ul>

        {{ range .Products }}

            <li>{{ . }}</li>

        {{ end }}

    </ul>

{{ else }}

    <p>No products available.</p>

{{ end }}
```

Nested Data Structures

If your data is hierarchical, you can use nested structs or maps.

Example:

go

```
type Product struct {

    Name   string

    Price float64

}
```

```go
type PageData struct {
    Title    string
    Heading  string
    Products []Product
}
```

Template:

html

```html
<ul>
    {{ range .Products }}
        <li>{{ .Name }} - ${{ .Price }}</li>
    {{ end }}
</ul>
```

Best Practices

1. **Keep Templates Simple**: Avoid complex logic in templates. Use Go code for processing.
2. **Sanitize Input**: Trust the `html/template` package to escape user-provided data.
3. **Cache Templates**: Parse templates once during application startup to optimize performance.

Hands-On Exercise

Objective

Create a dynamic webpage that displays a list of users and their roles.

Steps

1. Create a new template file, `users.html`:

html

```
<!DOCTYPE html>

<html lang="en">

<head>

    <meta charset="UTF-8">
```

```html
    <meta                           name="viewport"
content="width=device-width,            initial-
scale=1.0">

    <title>User List</title>

</head>

<body>

    <h1>Users</h1>

    <ul>

        {{ range . }}

            <li>{{   .Name   }}  -  {{   .Role
}}</li>

        {{ end }}

    </ul>

</body>

</html>
```

2. Update the Go code:

```go
type User struct {

    Name string

    Role string

}

func UserHandler(w http.ResponseWriter, r
*http.Request) {

    tmpl,                err              :=
template.ParseFiles("templates/users.html")

    if err != nil {

        http.Error(w,      "Error      loading
template", http.StatusInternalServerError)

        return

    }


    users := []User{
        {"Alice", "Admin"},
        {"Bob", "Editor"},
        {"Charlie", "Viewer"},
```

190

```go
    }

    tmpl.Execute(w, users)
}

func main() {

    http.HandleFunc("/users", UserHandler)

    http.ListenAndServe(":8080", nil)

}
```

3. Visit `http://localhost:8080/users` to view the dynamic user list.

4.3 Handling Forms and User Input

Forms are a fundamental part of web applications, enabling users to interact with your site by submitting data such as login credentials, search queries, or feedback. In this chapter, we'll explore how to handle forms and user input in Go, leveraging the `net/http` package and the `html/template` package for dynamic and secure web applications.

Understanding Forms and User Input

A form is an HTML element that collects user input and sends it to the server for processing. The server processes the submitted data, which can then be used to perform actions like saving to a database or rendering dynamic content.

HTML Form Basics

A simple form consists of input fields and a submit button, wrapped in a `<form>` tag.

Example:

html

```
<form action="/submit" method="POST">

    <label for="name">Name:</label>

    <input type="text" id="name" name="name"
required>

    <br>

    <label for="email">Email:</label>

    <input        type="email"        id="email"
name="email" required>
```

```
<br>

<button type="submit">Submit</button>
```

```
</form>
```

Key attributes:

- `action`: Specifies the URL to which the form data is sent.
- `method`: Defines the HTTP method (e.g., GET or POST) used to submit the form.

Handling Form Submissions in Go

Step 1: Create the Form Template

Create a folder named `templates` and add a file called `form.html`:

html

```
<!DOCTYPE html>

<html lang="en">

<head>

    <meta charset="UTF-8">
```

```html
    <meta                          name="viewport"
content="width=device-width,        initial-
scale=1.0">

    <title>Submit Form</title>

</head>

<body>

    <h1>Submit Your Information</h1>

    <form action="/submit" method="POST">

        <label for="name">Name:</label>

        <input      type="text"      id="name"
name="name" required>

        <br>

        <label for="email">Email:</label>

        <input     type="email"     id="email"
name="email" required>

        <br>

        <button
type="submit">Submit</button>

    </form>
```

```
</body>

</html>
```

Step 2: Write the Go Code

```go
package main

import (

    "fmt"

    "html/template"

    "net/http"

)

// RenderForm displays the HTML form

func RenderForm(w http.ResponseWriter, r
*http.Request) {

    tmpl,            err            :=
template.ParseFiles("templates/form.html")

    if err != nil {

        http.Error(w,    "Error    loading
template", http.StatusInternalServerError)
```

```go
        return
    }
    tmpl.Execute(w, nil)
}

// HandleSubmit processes the submitted form
data

func HandleSubmit(w http.ResponseWriter, r
*http.Request) {
    // Ensure the request method is POST
    if r.Method != http.MethodPost {
        http.Error(w,    "Invalid    request
method", http.StatusMethodNotAllowed)
        return
    }
    // Parse the form data
    err := r.ParseForm()
    if err != nil {
        http.Error(w,  "Error  parsing  form
data", http.StatusInternalServerError)
```

```go
        return

    }

    // Retrieve form values

    name := r.FormValue("name")

    email := r.FormValue("email")


    // Display the submitted data

    fmt.Fprintf(w,      "Form      submitted
successfully!<br>")

    fmt.Fprintf(w, "Name: %s<br>", name)

    fmt.Fprintf(w, "Email: %s<br>", email)

}


func main() {

    http.HandleFunc("/", RenderForm)

    http.HandleFunc("/submit", HandleSubmit)

    http.ListenAndServe(":8080", nil)

}
```

Detailed Explanation

1. **RenderForm Function**
   - Displays the form by parsing and executing the `form.html` template.

2. **HandleSubmit Function**
   - Validates that the request method is `POST` to ensure form data is submitted correctly.
   - Uses `r.ParseForm()` to parse the submitted form data.
   - Retrieves individual form values using `r.FormValue()`.

3. **Routing**
   - The root URL (`/`) serves the form.
   - The `/submit` endpoint processes the submitted data.

4. **Running the Application**
   - Start the server with `go run main.go`.
   - Visit `http://localhost:8080` to view the form.

Enhancing the Form

Adding More Input Fields

Expand the form to include additional fields like age and message:

html

```html
<label for="age">Age:</label>

<input type="number" id="age" name="age" required>

<br>

<label for="message">Message:</label>

<textarea id="message" name="message"></textarea>

<br>
```

Update the Go code to handle these fields:

go

```go
age := r.FormValue("age")

message := r.FormValue("message")

fmt.Fprintf(w, "Age: %s<br>", age)

fmt.Fprintf(w, "Message: %s<br>", message)
```

Security Considerations

1. **Validate Input**

   Always validate user input to ensure it meets the expected format.

2. **Escape Output**

   Use the `html/template` package to automatically escape user-provided data, preventing XSS attacks.

3. **CSRF Protection**

   Protect your forms from Cross-Site Request Forgery (CSRF) by using tokens.

Hands-On Exercise

Objective

Create a form to collect user feedback and display a thank-you message upon submission.

Steps

1. **Create the Template**

Save the following as `feedback.html`:

html

```
<!DOCTYPE html>

<html lang="en">
```

```html
<head>

    <meta charset="UTF-8">

    <meta                       name="viewport"
content="width=device-width,        initial-
scale=1.0">

    <title>Feedback</title>

</head>

<body>

    <h1>Submit Your Feedback</h1>

    <form action="/feedback" method="POST">

        <label for="name">Name:</label>

        <input      type="text"       id="name"
name="name" required>

        <br>

        <label
for="feedback">Feedback:</label>

        <textarea               id="feedback"
name="feedback" required></textarea>

        <br>
```

```html
        <button
type="submit">Submit</button>

    </form>

</body>

</html>
```

2. Update the Go Code

go

```go
func FeedbackHandler(w http.ResponseWriter, r
*http.Request) {

    if r.Method == http.MethodPost {

        err := r.ParseForm()

        if err != nil {

            http.Error(w,   "Error   parsing
form data", http.StatusInternalServerError)

            return

        }


        name := r.FormValue("name")
```

```go
    feedback := r.FormValue("feedback")

    fmt.Fprintf(w, "Thank you for your
feedback, %s!<br>", name)

    fmt.Fprintf(w, "Your message:
%s<br>", feedback)

    return

  }


  tmpl, err :=
template.ParseFiles("templates/feedback.html
")

  if err != nil {

    http.Error(w, "Error loading
template", http.StatusInternalServerError)

    return

  }

  tmpl.Execute(w, nil)

}
```

```go
func main() {

    http.HandleFunc("/feedback",
FeedbackHandler)

    http.ListenAndServe(":8080", nil)

}
```

3. **Test the Application**
    - Visit `http://localhost:8080/feedback`.
    - Submit the form and verify the thank-you message.

4.4 Building a Simple Blog Template

A blog is one of the most common examples of a dynamic web application. It displays content fetched from a data source, such as a database or in-memory storage, and allows for interaction through features like comments or search functionality. In this chapter, we will create a simple blog template using Go's `html/template` package to dynamically render content.

Understanding the Blog Structure

Before diving into code, let's outline the structure of our blog.

- **Homepage**: Displays a list of blog posts with titles and excerpts.
- **Post Page**: Shows the full content of a selected blog post.

For simplicity, we'll use a Go slice to store blog posts. Each post will have the following fields:

- `ID`: A unique identifier for the post.
- `Title`: The title of the post.
- `Content`: The full content of the post.
- `Excerpt`: A short preview of the content.

Step 1: Setting Up the Project

Project Structure

plaintext

```
blog/

├── templates/

│   ├── index.html

│   ├── post.html

├── main.go
```

Templates Folder

The `templates` folder will store our HTML files for the blog pages.

Step 2: Create the Data Model

Define a `Post` struct to represent a blog post:

go

```
package main

type Post struct {
    ID      int

    Title   string

    Content string

    Excerpt string
}
```

Create a slice to hold some sample posts:

go

```
var posts = []Post{
```

```
    {ID: 1, Title: "Introduction to Go",
Content: "Go is a statically typed, compiled
programming language designed for simplicity
and performance.", Excerpt: "Go is a
statically typed, compiled programming
language..."},

    {ID: 2, Title: "Understanding
Goroutines", Content: "Goroutines are
lightweight threads managed by the Go
runtime. They are a powerful tool for
concurrent programming.", Excerpt:
"Goroutines are lightweight threads..."},

    {ID: 3, Title: "Building Web Applications
with Go", Content: "Go's standard library
provides robust tools for building web
applications. Learn how to use the net/http
package effectively.", Excerpt: "Go's
standard library provides robust tools..."},

}
```

Step 3: Create the Templates

Homepage Template (`index.html`)

html

```html
<!DOCTYPE html>

<html lang="en">

<head>

    <meta charset="UTF-8">

    <meta                        name="viewport"
content="width=device-width,          initial-
scale=1.0">

    <title>Blog Homepage</title>

</head>

<body>

    <h1>Welcome to My Blog</h1>

    <ul>

        {{range .}}

        <li>

            <h2><a
href="/post/{{.ID}}">{{.Title}}</a></h2>

            <p>{{.Excerpt}}</p>
```

```
        </li>

        {{end}}

    </ul>

</body>

</html>
```

Post Page Template (`post.html`)

html

```
<!DOCTYPE html>

<html lang="en">

<head>

    <meta charset="UTF-8">

    <meta                        name="viewport"
content="width=device-width,        initial-
scale=1.0">

    <title>{{.Title}}</title>

</head>

<body>
```

```html
    <h1>{{.Title}}</h1>

    <p>{{.Content}}</p>

    <a href="/">Back to Homepage</a>

</body>

</html>
```

Step 4: Implement the Handlers

Homepage Handler

go

```go
package main

import (

    "html/template"

    "net/http"

)

func renderHomepage(w http.ResponseWriter, r
*http.Request) {

    tmpl,              err              :=
template.ParseFiles("templates/index.html")
```

```go
    if err != nil {

        http.Error(w,     "Error     loading
template", http.StatusInternalServerError)

        return

    }

    tmpl.Execute(w, posts)

}
```

Post Page Handler

go

```go
func   renderPost(w   http.ResponseWriter,   r
*http.Request) {

    // Extract the post ID from the URL

    id := r.URL.Path[len("/post/"):]

    for _, post := range posts {

        if fmt.Sprintf("%d", post.ID) == id
{

            tmpl,              err              :=
template.ParseFiles("templates/post.html")
```

```go
        if err != nil {
            http.Error(w,        "Error
loading                      template",
http.StatusInternalServerError)

            return

        }

        tmpl.Execute(w, post)

        return

    }

  }

  http.NotFound(w, r)

}
```

Step 5: Set Up Routing

go

```go
func main() {

    http.HandleFunc("/", renderHomepage)

    http.HandleFunc("/post/", renderPost)
```

```
// Start the server

http.ListenAndServe(":8080", nil)

}
```

Detailed Explanation

1. **Homepage Template**
   - Uses `{{range .}}` to iterate over the slice of posts and display each one.
   - Each title links to the corresponding post page using the post ID.
2. **Post Page Template**
   - Displays the full content of a single post.
   - Includes a back button linking to the homepage.
3. **Handlers**
   - `renderHomepage` renders the list of posts by passing the `posts` slice to the `index.html` template.
   - `renderPost` extracts the post ID from the URL and searches for the corresponding post in the `posts` slice.
4. **Routing**
   - `/`: Renders the homepage.

- ○ `/post/{id}`: Renders the individual post page.

Step 6: Run the Application

1. Save the code in `main.go`.

Run the application:
bash

```
go run main.go
```

2. Open `http://localhost:8080` in your browser to view the homepage.
3. Click on a post title to view its details.

Enhancements

1. **Pagination**
   Add pagination to the homepage to handle a large number of posts.
2. **Dynamic Data Source**
   Replace the in-memory slice with a database for persistent storage.
3. **Search Functionality**
   Add a search bar to filter posts by title or content.

Hands-On Exercise: Create a dynamic webpage that displays a list of blog posts fetched from a Go slice.

In this exercise, we will create a dynamic webpage using Go to display a list of blog posts fetched from a Go slice. This project will solidify your understanding of dynamic content rendering, routing, and working with templates in Go.

Project Overview

We aim to build a simple web application that:

1. Displays a list of blog posts on the homepage.
2. Allows users to click on a post title to view the full content of the post.

For simplicity, we'll use an in-memory Go slice to store blog posts.

Step 1: Setting Up the Project

Directory Structure

plaintext

```
blog/
├── templates/
```

```
|    ├── index.html

|    ├── post.html

├── main.go
```

- **templates/**: Contains HTML templates for the homepage and individual post pages.
- **main.go**: The main application file.

Step 2: Defining the Data Model

Create a Post Struct

In `main.go`, define a `Post` struct to represent a blog post:

```go
package main

type Post struct {
    ID      int

    Title   string

    Content string

    Excerpt string
```

216

```go
}
```

Initialize Sample Data

Create a slice of Post objects to simulate a database:

go

```go
var posts = []Post{
    {ID: 1, Title: "Introduction to Go",
Content: "Go is a statically typed, compiled
programming language designed for simplicity
and performance.", Excerpt: "Go is a
statically typed, compiled programming
language..."},

    {ID: 2, Title: "Understanding
Goroutines", Content: "Goroutines are
lightweight threads managed by the Go
runtime. They are a powerful tool for
concurrent programming.", Excerpt:
"Goroutines are lightweight threads..."},

    {ID: 3, Title: "Building Web Applications
with Go", Content: "Go's standard library
provides robust tools for building web
applications. Learn how to use the net/http
```

```
package    effectively.",    Excerpt:    "Go's
standard library provides robust tools..."},
```

```
}
```

Step 3: Creating Templates

Homepage Template (`index.html`)

This template displays a list of blog posts:

html

```
<!DOCTYPE html>

<html lang="en">

<head>

    <meta charset="UTF-8">

    <meta                     name="viewport"
content="width=device-width,         initial-
scale=1.0">

    <title>Blog Homepage</title>

</head>

<body>

    <h1>Welcome to My Blog</h1>
```

```
    <ul>

        {{range .}}

        <li>

            <h2><a
href="/post/{{.ID}}">{{.Title}}</a></h2>

            <p>{{.Excerpt}}</p>

        </li>

        {{end}}

    </ul>

</body>

</html>
```

- **Explanation**:
  - `{{range .}}` iterates over the list of posts.
  - Each post's title links to its detailed page using the ID.

Post Page Template (`post.html`)

This template displays the full content of a blog post:

html

```
<!DOCTYPE html>
```

```html
<html lang="en">

<head>

    <meta charset="UTF-8">

    <meta                    name="viewport"
content="width=device-width,        initial-
scale=1.0">

    <title>{{.Title}}</title>

</head>

<body>

    <h1>{{.Title}}</h1>

    <p>{{.Content}}</p>

    <a href="/">Back to Homepage</a>

</body>

</html>
```

- **Explanation**:
  - {{.Title}} and {{.Content}} display the post's title and content, respectively.
  - A link is provided to navigate back to the homepage.

Step 4: Writing Handlers

Homepage Handler

This handler renders the list of posts:

go

```go
package main

import (

    "html/template"

    "net/http"

)

func renderHomepage(w http.ResponseWriter, r *http.Request) {

    tmpl, err := template.ParseFiles("templates/index.html")

    if err != nil {

        http.Error(w, "Error loading template", http.StatusInternalServerError)

        return

    }
```

```go
    tmpl.Execute(w, posts)

}
```

Post Page Handler

This handler displays the full content of a specific post:

go

```go
func renderPost(w http.ResponseWriter, r
*http.Request) {

    id := r.URL.Path[len("/post/"):]

    for _, post := range posts {

        if fmt.Sprintf("%d", post.ID) == id {

            tmpl, err :=
template.ParseFiles("templates/post.html")

            if err != nil {

                http.Error(w, "Error loading
template", http.StatusInternalServerError)

                return

            }

            tmpl.Execute(w, post)

            return
```

```go
        }
    }
    http.NotFound(w, r)
}
```

- **Explanation**:
  - Extracts the post ID from the URL.
  - Searches for the post in the posts slice.
  - Renders the post.html template if the post is found.

Step 5: Setting Up Routes

Configure routes for the application:

go

```go
func main() {
    http.HandleFunc("/", renderHomepage)
    http.HandleFunc("/post/", renderPost)
    // Start the server
    http.ListenAndServe(":8080", nil)
}
```

- **Explanation**:

223

- o `/`: Renders the homepage.
- o `/post/{id}`: Displays the post page for a given ID.

Step 6: Running the Application

1. Save all files in their respective directories.

Run the application:
bash

```
go run main.go
```

2. Open your browser and navigate to `http://localhost:8080`.

Testing the Application

1. **Homepage**:
   - o Verify that the homepage displays the list of blog posts.
   - o Ensure each title links to the correct post page.
2. **Post Pages**:
   - o Click on a post title to view its details.
   - o Check that the content matches the data in the `posts` slice.

Enhancements

1. **Styling**: Add CSS to improve the appearance of the pages.
2. **Pagination**: Implement pagination for the homepage if there are many posts.
3. **Dynamic Data Source**: Replace the in-memory slice with a database for persistent storage.
4. **Search Functionality**: Add a search bar to filter posts by title or content.

Chapter 5: Building RESTful APIs

APIs (Application Programming Interfaces) are the backbone of modern web applications, enabling communication between different software systems. In this chapter, we'll explore the principles of RESTful API design, create CRUD endpoints in Go, work with JSON data, and test APIs using Postman.

By the end of this chapter, you'll have the knowledge and tools to build a RESTful API for a task management application, which will serve as a practical demonstration of the concepts covered.

5.1 Principles of RESTful API Design

RESTful APIs (Representational State Transfer APIs) are a fundamental part of modern web development. They provide a standardized way for applications to communicate, making them crucial for building scalable and maintainable systems. In this chapter, we will explore the principles of RESTful API design, their importance, and how to apply them effectively.

What is a RESTful API?

A RESTful API is an interface that adheres to the principles of REST architecture. It uses HTTP protocols to enable seamless communication between a client (e.g., a web browser or mobile app) and a server.

Core Characteristics of RESTful APIs

- **Stateless:** Each request from a client must contain all the information needed for the server to fulfill the request.
- **Resource-Oriented**: Everything is treated as a resource (e.g., users, tasks, products).
- **Uniform Interface**: Consistent use of HTTP methods (GET, POST, PUT, DELETE) and status codes.
- **Representation**: Resources are represented in standard formats like JSON or XML.

Principles of RESTful API Design

1. Resource Identification

Resources are the building blocks of RESTful APIs. They are typically represented by nouns and identified using URIs.

Example:

- A resource for tasks might have the URI `/tasks`.
- A specific task might be identified by `/tasks/1`.

2. HTTP Methods

RESTful APIs use HTTP methods to perform actions on resources.

227

HTTP Method	Description	Example
GET	Retrieve a resource.	/tasks
POST	Create a new resource.	/tasks
PUT	Update an existing resource.	/tasks/1
DELETE	Remove a resource.	/tasks/1

3. Statelessness

Each API request should be independent and contain all necessary information (e.g., authentication tokens, parameters).

Why It Matters:

Statelessness ensures scalability since the server doesn't need to maintain client-specific sessions.

4. Layered System

A RESTful API should be designed so that its client does not need to know about the server's internal structure. This abstraction allows for flexibility and scalability.

5. Cacheability

Responses should indicate whether they can be cached to improve performance and reduce server load. Use HTTP headers like `Cache-Control` and `ETag` to manage caching.

6. Uniform Interface

A consistent and predictable interface makes APIs easier to use and understand. This includes:

- Using plural nouns for resources (`/tasks` instead of `/task`).
- Standardizing response formats (e.g., always returning JSON).

7. Error Handling

Use HTTP status codes to indicate the result of an API call.

Status Code	Meaning	Example Scenario
`200 OK`	Request succeeded.	Successfully retrieved tasks.

201 Created	Resource created.	Successfully added a new task.
400 Bad Request	Invalid request.	Missing required parameters.
404 Not Found	Resource not found.	Task with specified ID doesn't exist.
500 Internal Server Error	Server error.	Unexpected server issue.

8. Versioning

Version your API to ensure backward compatibility.

Example:

- `/v1/tasks` for version 1.
- `/v2/tasks` for version 2 with updated functionality.

Best Practices for RESTful API Design

Use Meaningful URIs

URIs should be intuitive and self-explanatory.

Good Example:

plaintext

```
GET /users/123/tasks
```

Bad Example:

plaintext

```
GET /fetchTasksForUser?userId=123
```

Consistent Naming Conventions

Use lowercase letters and hyphens to separate words in URIs.

Example:

plaintext

```
GET /user-profiles
```

Paginate Large Datasets

For resources with large datasets, implement pagination to improve performance.

Example:

plaintext

```
GET /tasks?page=1&limit=10
```

Provide Detailed Documentation

Clear documentation with examples and explanations makes your API accessible to developers.

Practical Example: Designing a RESTful API for a Task Management System

Use Case

We want to design an API to manage tasks. Each task has the following attributes:

- `ID` (integer): Unique identifier.
- `Title` (string): Name of the task.
- `Description` (string): Details about the task.
- `Completed` (boolean): Status of the task.

API Endpoints

HTTP Method	URI	Description
GET	/tasks	Retrieve all tasks.
POST	/tasks	Create a new task.
GET	/tasks/{id}	Retrieve a specific task.
PUT	/tasks/{id}	Update a specific task.
DELETE	/tasks/{id}	Delete a specific task.

Sample JSON Response

json

```
{

  "id": 1,

  "title": "Learn Go",
```

```
  "description": "Study the Go programming
language",

  "completed": false

}
```

Exercise: Define Your Own RESTful API

1. Identify a resource in your application (e.g., products, orders).
2. Design a set of endpoints for CRUD operations.
3. Specify the request and response formats.
4. Consider edge cases (e.g., invalid inputs, resource not found).

5.2 Creating CRUD Endpoints in Go

CRUD (Create, Read, Update, Delete) operations are the backbone of most web applications. In this chapter, we will learn how to implement these operations in Go to manage resources in a RESTful API. We'll create a simple task management API to demonstrate each step, ensuring clarity and practicality.

Setting Up the Project

1. Initialize a New Go Project

Start by creating a new directory for your project and initializing it as a Go module.

bash

```
mkdir task-api

cd task-api

go mod init task-api
```

2. Install Necessary Packages

For simplicity, we'll use Go's standard `net/http` package. Optionally, you can install `gorilla/mux` for advanced routing.

bash

```
go get -u github.com/gorilla/mux
```

Designing the Task Resource

Each task will have the following attributes:

- `ID` (integer): Unique identifier.
- `Title` (string): Name of the task.

235

- Description (string): Details about the task.
- Completed (boolean): Status of the task.

Define a struct to represent a task:

go

```go
package main

type Task struct {
    ID          int     `json:"id"`
    Title       string  `json:"title"`
    Description string  `json:"description"`
    Completed   bool    `json:"completed"`
}
```

We'll also use a slice to store tasks in memory (for simplicity):

go

```go
var tasks []Task
var nextID = 1
```

Implementing CRUD Endpoints

1. Create (POST)

This endpoint allows clients to create a new task.

go

```go
func createTask(w http.ResponseWriter, r *http.Request) {

    var newTask Task

    err := json.NewDecoder(r.Body).Decode(&newTask)

    if err != nil {

        http.Error(w, "Invalid input", http.StatusBadRequest)

        return

    }


    newTask.ID = nextID

    nextID++

    tasks = append(tasks, newTask)
```

```go
    w.WriteHeader(http.StatusCreated)

    json.NewEncoder(w).Encode(newTask)

}
```

2. Read (GET)

a. Get All Tasks

go

```go
func    getTasks(w    http.ResponseWriter,    r
*http.Request) {

    json.NewEncoder(w).Encode(tasks)

}
```

b. Get a Specific Task

go

```go
func    getTaskByID(w    http.ResponseWriter,    r
*http.Request) {

    params := mux.Vars(r)

    id, err := strconv.Atoi(params["id"])
```

```go
    if err != nil {

        http.Error(w,      "Invalid      ID",
http.StatusBadRequest)

        return

    }


    for _, task := range tasks {

        if task.ID == id {

            json.NewEncoder(w).Encode(task)

            return

        }

    }


    http.Error(w,    "Task    not    found",
http.StatusNotFound)

}
```

3. Update (PUT)

This endpoint updates an existing task by ID.

```go
func updateTask(w http.ResponseWriter, r
*http.Request) {

    params := mux.Vars(r)

    id, err := strconv.Atoi(params["id"])

    if err != nil {

        http.Error(w,        "Invalid        ID",
http.StatusBadRequest)

        return

    }

    var updatedTask Task

    err                                       =
json.NewDecoder(r.Body).Decode(&updatedTask)

    if err != nil {

        http.Error(w,      "Invalid      input",
http.StatusBadRequest)

        return

    }

    for i, task := range tasks {
```
240

```
        if task.ID == id {

            tasks[i].Title                =
updatedTask.Title

            tasks[i].Description          =
updatedTask.Description

            tasks[i].Completed            =
updatedTask.Completed


json.NewEncoder(w).Encode(tasks[i])

            return

        }

    }

    http.Error(w,    "Task    not    found",
http.StatusNotFound)

}
```

4. Delete (DELETE)

This endpoint deletes a task by ID.

```go
func deleteTask(w http.ResponseWriter, r *http.Request) {

    params := mux.Vars(r)

    id, err := strconv.Atoi(params["id"])

    if err != nil {

        http.Error(w, "Invalid ID", http.StatusBadRequest)

        return

    }


    for i, task := range tasks {

        if task.ID == id {

            tasks = append(tasks[:i], tasks[i+1:]...)

w.WriteHeader(http.StatusNoContent)

            return

        }
```

```go
    }

    http.Error(w,    "Task    not    found",
http.StatusNotFound)

}
```

Setting Up Routes

Use the `gorilla/mux` router to define routes for each endpoint.

go

```go
func main() {

    router := mux.NewRouter()

    router.HandleFunc("/tasks",
createTask).Methods("POST")

    router.HandleFunc("/tasks",
getTasks).Methods("GET")

    router.HandleFunc("/tasks/{id}",
getTaskByID).Methods("GET")

    router.HandleFunc("/tasks/{id}",
updateTask).Methods("PUT")
```

```
    router.HandleFunc("/tasks/{id}",
deleteTask).Methods("DELETE")


    fmt.Println("Server is running on port
8080")

    http.ListenAndServe(":8080", router)

}
```

Testing the API

Run the Server
Compile and run the application:
bash

```
go run main.go
```

1. **Use Postman or cURL**

Create a Task:
bash

```
curl -X POST -H "Content-Type:
application/json" -d '{"title":"Learn
Go","description":"Study Go
```

```
programming","completed":false}'
http://localhost:8080/tasks
```

○

Get All Tasks:
bash

```
curl http://localhost:8080/tasks
```

Update a Task:
bash

```
curl -X PUT -H "Content-Type:
application/json" -d '{"title":"Learn
GoLang","description":"Master Go
programming","completed":true}'
http://localhost:8080/tasks/1
```

Delete a Task:
bash

```
curl -X DELETE http://localhost:8080/tasks/1
```

5.3 Working with JSON Data

JSON (JavaScript Object Notation) is a lightweight data-interchange format widely used in RESTful APIs for its simplicity and readability. In Go, the `encoding/json` package provides robust tools for encoding and decoding JSON data. This chapter covers how to work with JSON in Go, including serializing and deserializing data, handling errors, and using JSON effectively in APIs.

Understanding JSON in Go

JSON represents data as key-value pairs, arrays, or nested objects. Here's an example of JSON data:

json

```json
{

    "id": 1,

    "title": "Learn Go",

    "description": "Master the Go programming
language",

    "completed": false

}
```

In Go, JSON data is typically mapped to structs for easy manipulation.

Serializing Data to JSON

Serialization (or marshalling) converts Go data structures into JSON format.

Example: Converting a Struct to JSON

go

```go
package main

import (

    "encoding/json"

    "fmt"

)


type Task struct {

    ID          int     `json:"id"`

    Title       string `json:"title"`

    Description string `json:"description"`

    Completed   bool    `json:"completed"`
```

```go
}

func main() {
    task := Task{
        ID:          1,
        Title:       "Learn Go",
        Description: "Master   the   Go
programming language",
        Completed:   false,
    }

    jsonData, err := json.Marshal(task)
    if err != nil {
        fmt.Println("Error      marshalling
JSON:", err)
        return
    }

    fmt.Println(string(jsonData))
```

```
}
```

Output:

json

```
{"id":1,"title":"Learn
Go","description":"Master the Go programming
language","completed":false}
```

Customizing JSON Field Names

The struct tags (`json:"field_name"`) define how fields are serialized. For example, `json:"completed"` ensures the field `Completed` is serialized as `completed`.

Deserializing JSON to Go Structs

Deserialization (or unmarshalling) converts JSON data into Go data structures.

Example: Parsing JSON into a Struct

go

```
package main
```

```go
import (

    "encoding/json"

    "fmt"

)


type Task struct {

    ID          int    `json:"id"`

    Title       string `json:"title"`

    Description string `json:"description"`

    Completed   bool   `json:"completed"`

}


func main() {

    jsonData    :=    `{"id":1,"title":"Learn
Go","description":"Master the Go programming
language","completed":false}`


    var task Task
```

```go
    err := json.Unmarshal([]byte(jsonData),
&task)

    if err != nil {

        fmt.Println("Error     unmarshalling
JSON:", err)

        return

    }


    fmt.Printf("Task: %+v\n", task)

}
```

Output:

plaintext

```
Task: {ID:1 Title:Learn Go Description:Master
the Go programming language Completed:false}
```

Handling JSON Arrays

Go can handle JSON arrays by using slices.

Example: Parsing an Array of JSON Objects

go

```go
package main

import (

    "encoding/json"

    "fmt"

)

type Task struct {

    ID          int     `json:"id"`

    Title       string `json:"title"`

    Description string `json:"description"`

    Completed   bool    `json:"completed"`

}

func main() {

    jsonData := `[

        {"id":1,"title":"Learn
Go","description":"Master the Go programming
language","completed":false},
```

```go
        {"id":2,"title":"Build
API","description":"Create a RESTful API in
Go","completed":true}

    ]`


    var tasks []Task

    err := json.Unmarshal([]byte(jsonData),
&tasks)

    if err != nil {

        fmt.Println("Error      unmarshalling
JSON:", err)

        return

    }


    for _, task := range tasks {

        fmt.Printf("Task: %+v\n", task)

    }

}
```

Output:

plaintext

```
Task: {ID:1 Title:Learn Go Description:Master
the Go programming language Completed:false}

Task:       {ID:2       Title:Build        API
Description:Create   a   RESTful   API   in   Go
Completed:true}
```

Error Handling in JSON Operations

Always check for errors when marshalling or unmarshalling JSON. Common issues include:

1. Invalid JSON syntax.
2. Type mismatches between JSON and Go struct fields.
3. Missing or unexpected fields.

Example: Handling Missing Fields

go

```go
package main


import (

    "encoding/json"
```

```go
    "fmt"
)

type Task struct {
    ID          int    `json:"id"`
    Title       string `json:"title"`
    Description string `json:"description"`
    Completed   bool   `json:"completed"`
}

func main() {
    jsonData := `{"id":1,"title":"Learn Go"}`
    // Missing "description" and "completed"

    var task Task

    err := json.Unmarshal([]byte(jsonData), &task)

    if err != nil {

        fmt.Println("Error    unmarshalling JSON:", err)

        return

    }
```

```go
    fmt.Printf("Task: %+v\n", task)
}
```

Output:

plaintext

```
Task:  {ID:1  Title:Learn  Go  Description:
Completed:false}
```

Practical Example: Handling JSON in an API

Let's integrate JSON handling into a simple API.

Example: API Endpoint to Create a Task

go

```go
package main

import (

    "encoding/json"

    "fmt"

    "net/http"
```

```go
)

type Task struct {
    ID          int    `json:"id"`

    Title       string `json:"title"`

    Description string `json:"description"`

    Completed   bool   `json:"completed"`
}

var tasks []Task

var nextID = 1

func                          createTaskHandler(w
http.ResponseWriter, r *http.Request) {

    var newTask Task

    err                              :=
json.NewDecoder(r.Body).Decode(&newTask)

    if err != nil {

        http.Error(w, "Invalid JSON input",
http.StatusBadRequest)

        return

    }
```

```go
    newTask.ID = nextID

    nextID++

    tasks = append(tasks, newTask)


    w.WriteHeader(http.StatusCreated)

    json.NewEncoder(w).Encode(newTask)
}


func main() {

    http.HandleFunc("/tasks",
createTaskHandler)


    fmt.Println("Server        running        on
http://localhost:8080")

    http.ListenAndServe(":8080", nil)
}
```

Testing the Endpoint

Use cURL or Postman to test:

bash

```
curl -X POST -H "Content-Type:
application/json" -d '{"title":"Learn
Go","description":"Master
Go","completed":false}'
http://localhost:8080/tasks
```

Best Practices for Working with JSON

1. **Validate Input**: Always validate JSON input to ensure data integrity.
2. **Use Struct Tags**: Define clear struct tags for field mapping.
3. **Handle Errors Gracefully**: Provide meaningful error messages to clients.
4. **Optimize Performance**: Use streaming for large JSON data sets.

5.4 Testing APIs with Postman

Testing is a critical step in API development. Postman, a popular API testing tool, simplifies this process with its intuitive interface and robust features. This chapter introduces Postman, walks you through setting it up, and demonstrates how to test RESTful APIs effectively.

Why Use Postman?

Postman offers several advantages for API testing:

1. **User-Friendly Interface**: Easily send requests and view responses.
2. **Support for Multiple HTTP Methods**: Test GET, POST, PUT, DELETE, and more.
3. **Automation and Collaboration**: Save requests, create test collections, and share with teams.
4. **Detailed Response Analysis**: View headers, body, status codes, and response times.

Getting Started with Postman

Step 1: Download and Install Postman

1. Visit the Postman website and download the app for your platform (Windows, macOS, or Linux).
2. Install and launch the application.

Step 2: Create an Account

1. Sign up for a free account or log in if you already have one.
2. While an account is optional for basic use, it enables syncing and collaboration features.

Testing an API Endpoint

Example: Testing a GET Endpoint

Let's assume you have a running API with a GET /tasks endpoint that retrieves a list of tasks.

Server Code Example:

```go
package main

import (

    "encoding/json"

    "fmt"

    "net/http"

)


type Task struct {
```

```go
    ID          int     `json:"id"`

    Title       string `json:"title"`

    Description string `json:"description"`

    Completed   bool    `json:"completed"`
}

var tasks = []Task{

    {ID: 1, Title: "Learn Go", Description:
"Master Go programming", Completed: false},

    {ID: 2, Title: "Build API", Description:
"Create RESTful APIs in Go", Completed:
true},

}

func getTasksHandler(w http.ResponseWriter, r
*http.Request) {

    w.Header().Set("Content-Type",
"application/json")

    json.NewEncoder(w).Encode(tasks)

}

func main() {
```

```go
    http.HandleFunc("/tasks",
getTasksHandler)

    fmt.Println("Server        running        on
http://localhost:8080")

    http.ListenAndServe(":8080", nil)

}
```

1. Start the server using the code above.
2. Open Postman and create a new request.

Step 3: Sending a GET Request in Postman

1. Click + **New Tab** to open a new request.
2. Select **GET** as the HTTP method.
3. Enter the URL `http://localhost:8080/tasks`.
4. Click **Send**.

Expected Response:

json

```json
[

    {

        "id": 1,

        "title": "Learn Go",
```

```
      "description":        "Master        Go
programming",

      "completed": false

  },

  {

      "id": 2,

      "title": "Build API",

      "description": "Create  RESTful  APIs
in Go",

      "completed": true

  }

]
```

Testing a POST Endpoint

Example: Testing a POST Endpoint

Let's add a POST /tasks endpoint to create new tasks.

Server Code Update:

```go
func                    createTaskHandler(w
http.ResponseWriter, r *http.Request) {

    var newTask Task

    err                              :=
json.NewDecoder(r.Body).Decode(&newTask)

    if err != nil {

        http.Error(w, "Invalid JSON input",
http.StatusBadRequest)

        return

    }

    newTask.ID = len(tasks) + 1

    tasks = append(tasks, newTask)

    w.WriteHeader(http.StatusCreated)

    json.NewEncoder(w).Encode(newTask)

}

func main() {

    http.HandleFunc("/tasks",            func(w
http.ResponseWriter, r *http.Request) {
```

```go
        if r.Method == http.MethodGet {

            getTasksHandler(w, r)

        } else if r.Method == http.MethodPost
{

            createTaskHandler(w, r)

        } else {

            http.Error(w,    "Method    not
allowed", http.StatusMethodNotAllowed)

        }

    })

    fmt.Println("Server        running        on
http://localhost:8080")

    http.ListenAndServe(":8080", nil)

}
```

Step 1: Add a POST Request in Postman

1. Open a new request in Postman.
2. Select **POST** as the HTTP method.
3. Enter the URL `http://localhost:8080/tasks`.
4. Go to the **Body** tab, select **raw**, and choose **JSON** as the format.

5. Add the following JSON data:

json

```
{

    "title": "Write Book",

    "description":    "Complete    the    Go
programming book",

    "completed": false

}
```

6. Click **Send**.

Expected Response:

json

```
{

    "id": 3,

    "title": "Write Book",

    "description":    "Complete    the    Go
programming book",

    "completed": false

}
```

Analyzing API Responses

Postman displays detailed response data:

1. **Status Code**: Indicates success (e.g., `200 OK`) or failure (e.g., `400 Bad Request`).
2. **Response Body**: Shows the data returned by the server.
3. **Headers**: Displays metadata such as `Content-Type`.
4. **Response Time**: Measures the time taken by the server to respond.

Saving Requests and Creating Collections

Postman allows you to save requests for reuse:

1. Click **Save** after configuring a request.
2. Organize requests into collections for easy access.
3. Share collections with team members for collaboration.

Automating Tests with Postman

Postman supports automated testing using JavaScript snippets.

Example: Adding Tests to a Request

1. Go to the **Tests** tab in your request.

2. Add the following test script:

javascript

```
pm.test("Status code is 201", function () {
    pm.response.to.have.status(201);
});


pm.test("Response has ID", function () {
    const jsonData = pm.response.json();

    pm.expect(jsonData).to.have.property("id");
});
```

3. Send the request to see test results in the **Test Results** tab.

Best Practices for API Testing with Postman

1. **Use Collections**: Organize related requests for better management.

2. **Automate Tests**: Add test scripts to validate responses automatically.
3. **Environment Variables**: Use variables for URLs, tokens, and other dynamic data.
4. **Monitor Performance**: Analyze response times to identify bottlenecks.

Hands-On Project: Build a RESTful API for a task management application (e.g., To-Do List).

In this hands-on project, we will build a fully functional RESTful API for a task management application. This project will cover creating endpoints for CRUD (Create, Read, Update, Delete) operations, handling JSON data, and testing the API using Postman.

By the end of this project, you will have a clear understanding of how to design, build, and test a RESTful API using Go.

Project Overview

We will build an API with the following endpoints:

1. **GET /tasks**: Retrieve all tasks.
2. **GET /tasks/{id}**: Retrieve a specific task by ID.
3. **POST /tasks**: Create a new task.
4. **PUT /tasks/{id}**: Update an existing task.

5. **DELETE /tasks/{id}**: Delete a task by ID.

Each task will have the following fields:

- `ID` (integer): Unique identifier.
- `Title` (string): Task title.
- `Description` (string): Task description.
- `Completed` (boolean): Status of the task.

Step 1: Setting Up the Project

Create a New Go Project:

Open a terminal and create a new directory for your project:
bash

```
mkdir task-manager-api

cd task-manager-api

go mod init task-manager-api
```

Install Required Packages:

We will use the `gorilla/mux` package for routing. Install it using:
bash

```
go get -u github.com/gorilla/mux
```

Step 2: Define the Task Data Structure

Create a new file main.go and define the Task struct:

go

```go
package main

import (

    "encoding/json"

    "fmt"

    "net/http"

    "strconv"


    "github.com/gorilla/mux"
)

// Task represents a task in the application

type Task struct {

    ID          int     `json:"id"`

    Title       string `json:"title"`

    Description string `json:"description"`

    Completed   bool    `json:"completed"`
```

```
}

// In-memory task storage

var tasks []Task

var nextID = 1
```

Step 3: Create the API Endpoints

1. GET /tasks: Retrieve All Tasks

go

```go
func getTasksHandler(w http.ResponseWriter, r
*http.Request) {

    w.Header().Set("Content-Type",
"application/json")

    json.NewEncoder(w).Encode(tasks)

}
```

2. GET /tasks/{id}: Retrieve a Task by ID

go

```go
func getTaskHandler(w http.ResponseWriter, r
*http.Request) {
```

```go
    w.Header().Set("Content-Type",
"application/json")

    params := mux.Vars(r)

    id, err := strconv.Atoi(params["id"])

    if err != nil {

        http.Error(w, "Invalid task ID",
http.StatusBadRequest)

        return

    }

    for _, task := range tasks {

        if task.ID == id {

            json.NewEncoder(w).Encode(task)

            return

        }

    }


    http.Error(w, "Task not found",
http.StatusNotFound)

}
```

3. POST /tasks: Create a New Task

go

```go
func                    createTaskHandler(w
http.ResponseWriter, r *http.Request) {

    w.Header().Set("Content-Type",
"application/json")

    var newTask Task

    err                                 :=
json.NewDecoder(r.Body).Decode(&newTask)

    if err != nil {

        http.Error(w,    "Invalid    input",
http.StatusBadRequest)

        return

    }

    newTask.ID = nextID

    nextID++

    tasks = append(tasks, newTask)

    w.WriteHeader(http.StatusCreated)
```

```go
    json.NewEncoder(w).Encode(newTask)

}
```

4. PUT /tasks/{id}: Update an Existing Task

go

```go
func                    updateTaskHandler(w
http.ResponseWriter, r *http.Request) {

    w.Header().Set("Content-Type",
"application/json")

    params := mux.Vars(r)

    id, err := strconv.Atoi(params["id"])

    if err != nil {

        http.Error(w,  "Invalid  task  ID",
http.StatusBadRequest)

        return

    }

    for i, task := range tasks {

        if task.ID == id {

            var updatedTask Task
```

```go
        err :=
json.NewDecoder(r.Body).Decode(&updatedTask)

        if err != nil {

            http.Error(w,      "Invalid
input", http.StatusBadRequest)

            return

        }

        updatedTask.ID = id

        tasks[i] = updatedTask

    json.NewEncoder(w).Encode(updatedTask)

        return

        }

    }

    http.Error(w,   "Task    not    found",
http.StatusNotFound)

}
```

5. DELETE /tasks/{id}: Delete a Task

go

```go
func                    deleteTaskHandler(w
http.ResponseWriter, r *http.Request) {

    w.Header().Set("Content-Type",
"application/json")

    params := mux.Vars(r)

    id, err := strconv.Atoi(params["id"])

    if err != nil {

        http.Error(w,  "Invalid  task  ID",
http.StatusBadRequest)

        return

    }

    for i, task := range tasks {

        if task.ID == id {

            tasks    =    append(tasks[:i],
tasks[i+1:]...)


    w.WriteHeader(http.StatusNoContent)
```

278

```go
        return

    }

  }

  http.Error(w,    "Task    not    found",
http.StatusNotFound)

}
```

Step 4: Set Up Routing and Start the Server

Add the following code to set up routes and start the server:

go

```go
func main() {

    router := mux.NewRouter()

    // Define API routes

    router.HandleFunc("/tasks",
getTasksHandler).Methods("GET")

    router.HandleFunc("/tasks/{id}",
getTaskHandler).Methods("GET")

    router.HandleFunc("/tasks",
createTaskHandler).Methods("POST")
```

```go
    router.HandleFunc("/tasks/{id}",
updateTaskHandler).Methods("PUT")

    router.HandleFunc("/tasks/{id}",
deleteTaskHandler).Methods("DELETE")


    fmt.Println("Server          running          on
http://localhost:8080")

    http.ListenAndServe(":8080", router)

}
```

Step 5: Testing the API

Start the Server:
Run the application:
bash

```bash
go run main.go
```

1. **Test Using Postman:**
   ○ Use the **GET, POST, PUT**, and **DELETE** methods to interact with the API.
   ○ Verify responses and status codes for each endpoint.

Chapter 6: Database Integration

Databases are a critical component of most modern applications. They allow us to store, retrieve, and manage data efficiently. In this chapter, we will explore how to integrate databases with Go applications, covering both SQL and NoSQL databases, and using GORM, a popular Object-Relational Mapping (ORM) library.

We will also build a hands-on project that connects a Go application to a database to manage a list of products.

6.1 Introduction to SQL and NoSQL Databases

Databases are at the heart of most applications, serving as the backbone for storing, managing, and retrieving data. Whether you are building a simple website or a complex enterprise application, understanding the fundamentals of databases is crucial. In this section, we will dive into the two main types of databases: SQL (Structured Query Language) and NoSQL (Not Only SQL). We'll explore their differences, when to use each, and the scenarios where they shine.

What is a Database?

A database is an organized collection of data that can be easily accessed, managed, and updated. Databases are used in nearly every application, from e-commerce websites to mobile apps and enterprise systems.

They allow us to store large amounts of data in an efficient and structured way, making it easy to retrieve, update, and delete information as needed.

The two primary categories of databases are:

1. **SQL Databases**: These are relational databases that store data in tables with rows and columns. They use SQL for querying and managing data.
2. **NoSQL Databases**: These are non-relational databases that allow for flexible data models. They store data in formats like key-value pairs, documents, graphs, or wide-columns.

SQL Databases: Structured and Relational

SQL databases, also known as relational databases, organize data into structured tables. These tables have predefined columns with specific data types, and relationships can be established between different tables using keys. SQL databases use SQL to interact with the data, which is a powerful language for querying, updating, and managing data.

Key Features of SQL Databases:

1. Schema-based: SQL databases have a fixed schema that defines the structure of the data. Each table has a predefined set of columns with specified data types (e.g., INT, VARCHAR, DATE).

2. **ACID Properties**: SQL databases follow the ACID (Atomicity, Consistency, Isolation, Durability) properties to ensure data integrity. This makes them reliable for transactions.

3. **Data Relationships**: SQL databases support relationships between tables using keys, such as primary keys (PK) and foreign keys (FK). This is useful for modeling complex relationships.

4. **Examples**: PostgreSQL, MySQL, SQLite, Microsoft SQL Server.

When to Use SQL Databases:

- **Structured Data:** If your data has a clear structure and relationships (e.g., customer data, product catalogs, or financial records), SQL databases are ideal.

- **Transactions**: SQL databases are well-suited for applications that require strong consistency and transactional support (e.g., banking systems, e-commerce platforms).

- **Complex Queries**: SQL databases allow for complex queries using JOINs, GROUP BY, and other SQL operations, making them ideal for reporting and data analysis.

NoSQL Databases: Flexible and Scalable

NoSQL databases are designed for applications that require flexibility and scalability. Unlike SQL databases, NoSQL databases do not rely on a fixed schema, and they can handle a wide variety of data types and structures. They are often used in scenarios where performance, scalability, and flexibility are more important than strict data consistency.

Key Features of NoSQL Databases:

1. Schema-less: NoSQL databases do not require a predefined schema, allowing you to store data in various formats like JSON, BSON, or XML. This makes them more flexible for handling unstructured or semi-structured data.
2. **Scalability**: NoSQL databases are designed to scale horizontally, meaning they can handle large amounts of data and high traffic by distributing the load across multiple servers.
3. **Eventual Consistency**: Unlike SQL databases, which ensure strong consistency (ACID), NoSQL databases often follow the concept of eventual consistency, meaning data may not be immediately consistent across all nodes, but will eventually become consistent.
4. **Data Models**: NoSQL databases offer different data models:
   - **Document-Based**: Stores data as documents (e.g., MongoDB, CouchDB).
   - **Key-Value Stores**: Data is stored as key-value pairs (e.g., Redis, Riak).
   - **Column-Family Stores**: Data is stored in columns rather than rows (e.g., Cassandra, HBase).
   - **Graph Databases**: Data is stored as nodes and edges, ideal for graph-based relationships (e.g., Neo4j).

5. **Examples**: MongoDB, Cassandra, Redis, CouchDB, Neo4j.

When to Use NoSQL Databases:

- **Unstructured or Semi-structured Data**: If your data does not fit neatly into tables or requires flexibility (e.g., social media posts, logs, or sensor data), NoSQL databases are a good choice.
- **High Scalability**: NoSQL databases excel at scaling horizontally, making them ideal for applications that require handling large volumes of data and high traffic (e.g., real-time analytics, big data processing).
- **Rapid Development**: NoSQL databases allow for quick iteration and development since they do not require a fixed schema.

SQL vs. NoSQL: Which One Should You Choose?

When deciding between SQL and NoSQL, it's important to consider the specific needs of your application. Here's a quick comparison:

Feature	SQL Databases	NoSQL Databases
Data Structure	Structured (Tables, Rows, Columns)	Flexible (Documents, Key-Value, etc.)

Schema	Fixed Schema	Schema-less
Scalability	Vertical Scaling (Scaling up)	Horizontal Scaling (Scaling out)
Transactions	ACID-compliant (Strong Consistency)	Eventual Consistency (Tradeoff)
Use Cases	Financial Systems, CRM, ERP	Social Media, IoT, Real-Time Data
Examples	PostgreSQL, MySQL, SQL Server	MongoDB, Cassandra, Redis

Practical Exercise: Choosing the Right Database

Let's consider a scenario where you need to build a social media platform. The platform will store user data, posts, comments, and likes.

- **SQL Database**: If the data is highly structured and you need strong consistency (e.g., user profiles, transactional data), you might choose a SQL database like PostgreSQL.
- **NoSQL Database**: If the data is more flexible and you need to scale horizontally (e.g., storing posts, comments, and likes in a schema-less format), a NoSQL database like MongoDB might be a better choice.

6.2 Connecting Go to a Database (PostgreSQL, MySQL)

In modern web applications, databases play a vital role in storing, retrieving, and managing data. Go provides robust support for working with relational databases like PostgreSQL and MySQL through its `database/sql` package and third-party drivers. This chapter will guide you through connecting your Go application to PostgreSQL and MySQL, setting up a database connection, and performing basic operations like querying and inserting data.

Step 1: Setting Up Your Environment

Before diving into the code, ensure you have the following installed:

- **Go**: A recent version of the Go programming language.
- **Database Server**: PostgreSQL or MySQL installed on your local machine or a cloud instance.
- **Database Driver**: A Go driver for the respective database.

Installing Drivers

Use the following commands to install the required drivers:

PostgreSQL Driver:
bash

```
go get github.com/lib/pq
```

MySQL Driver:
bash

```
go get github.com/go-sql-driver/mysql
```

Step 2: Configuring the Database

PostgreSQL Configuration

1. Start your PostgreSQL server.

Create a database and a table for demonstration:
sql

```
CREATE DATABASE mydb;

\c mydb

CREATE TABLE users (
```

```sql
    id SERIAL PRIMARY KEY,

    name VARCHAR(100),

    email VARCHAR(100)

);
```

MySQL Configuration

1. Start your MySQL server.

Create a database and a table:
sql

```sql
CREATE DATABASE mydb;

USE mydb;

CREATE TABLE users (

    id INT AUTO_INCREMENT PRIMARY KEY,

    name VARCHAR(100),

    email VARCHAR(100)

);
```

Step 3: Writing Go Code to Connect to the Database

PostgreSQL Connection

```go
package main

import (

    "database/sql"

    "fmt"

    "log"


    _ "github.com/lib/pq"

)


func main() {
    // Connection string

    connStr := "user=yourusername password=yourpassword dbname=mydb sslmode=disable"

    db, err := sql.Open("postgres", connStr)
```

```go
    if err != nil {

        log.Fatalf("Unable to connect to
database: %v", err)

    }

    defer db.Close()


    // Test the connection

    err = db.Ping()

    if err != nil {

        log.Fatalf("Ping failed: %v", err)

    }

    fmt.Println("Connected to PostgreSQL
database!")

}
```

MySQL Connection

go

```go
package main
```

```go
import (

    "database/sql"

    "fmt"

    "log"


    _ "github.com/go-sql-driver/mysql"

)


func main() {

    // Connection string

    connStr                            :=
"yourusername:yourpassword@tcp(127.0.0.1:330
6)/mydb"

    db, err := sql.Open("mysql", connStr)

    if err != nil {

        log.Fatalf("Unable   to   connect   to
database: %v", err)

    }

    defer db.Close()
```

```go
    // Test the connection

    err = db.Ping()

    if err != nil {

        log.Fatalf("Ping failed: %v", err)

    }

    fmt.Println("Connected      to      MySQL
database!")

}
```

Step 4: Performing Basic Database Operations

Inserting Data

go

```go
func insertUser(db *sql.DB, name, email
string) {

    query := "INSERT INTO users (name, email)
VALUES ($1, $2)" // Use `?` placeholders for
MySQL

    _, err := db.Exec(query, name, email)
```

```go
    if err != nil {

        log.Fatalf("Error  inserting  data:
%v", err)

    }

    fmt.Println("User                inserted
successfully!")

}
```

Querying Data

```go
func fetchUsers(db *sql.DB) {

    query := "SELECT id, name, email FROM
users"

    rows, err := db.Query(query)

    if err != nil {

        log.Fatalf("Error  fetching  data:
%v", err)

    }

    defer rows.Close()
```

```go
    for rows.Next() {

        var id int

        var name, email string

        err := rows.Scan(&id, &name, &email)

        if err != nil {

            log.Fatalf("Error scanning row:
%v", err)

        }

        fmt.Printf("ID: %d, Name: %s, Email:
%s\n", id, name, email)

    }

}
```

Example Usage

go

```go
func main() {

    // Connect to the database (PostgreSQL
example)
```

```go
    connStr := "user=yourusername password=yourpassword dbname=mydb sslmode=disable"

    db, err := sql.Open("postgres", connStr)

    if err != nil {

        log.Fatalf("Unable to connect to database: %v", err)

    }

    defer db.Close()


    // Insert a user

    insertUser(db, "John Doe", "john.doe@example.com")


    // Fetch all users

    fetchUsers(db)
}
```

Step 5: Best Practices

1. **Environment Variables**: Store sensitive information like credentials in environment variables or a configuration file.
2. **Connection Pooling**: Use connection pooling to manage database connections efficiently.
3. **Error Handling**: Always check for errors and handle them appropriately.
4. **Prepared Statements**: Use prepared statements to prevent SQL injection.

6.3 Using GORM for Simplified Database Operations

Managing database interactions in Go can be tedious using raw SQL and the `database/sql` package. **GORM**, a powerful ORM (Object-Relational Mapper) for Go, simplifies database operations by providing an abstraction layer over SQL. It supports advanced features like migrations, associations, and query building, making it an excellent choice for developers looking to streamline database interactions.

This chapter will introduce GORM, demonstrate how to integrate it into your Go project, and show you how to perform common database operations.

Step 1: Installing GORM

To use GORM, install the library and the corresponding database driver. For example:

PostgreSQL:
bash

```
go        get        -u        gorm.io/gorm
gorm.io/driver/postgres
```

MySQL:
bash

```
go get -u gorm.io/gorm gorm.io/driver/mysql
```

Step 2: Setting Up GORM

PostgreSQL Example

go

```
package main

import (

    "gorm.io/driver/postgres"
```

```go
    "gorm.io/gorm"

    "log"

)

func main() {

    dsn := "user=yourusername password=yourpassword dbname=mydb sslmode=disable"

    db, err := gorm.Open(postgres.Open(dsn), &gorm.Config{})

    if err != nil {

        log.Fatalf("Failed to connect to database: %v", err)

    }


    log.Println("Connected to PostgreSQL database using GORM!")

}
```

MySQL Example

go

```
package main

import (

    "gorm.io/driver/mysql"

    "gorm.io/gorm"

    "log"

)

func main() {

    dsn                              :=
"yourusername:yourpassword@tcp(127.0.0.1:330
6)/mydb"

    db,  err  :=  gorm.Open(mysql.Open(dsn),
&gorm.Config{})

    if err != nil {

        log.Fatalf("Failed  to  connect  to
database: %v", err)

    }
```

```go
    log.Println("Connected to MySQL database
using GORM!")

}
```

Step 3: Defining Models

In GORM, a **model** represents a database table. Define a User model to represent the users table:

go

```go
package main

import (

    "gorm.io/gorm"

)

type User struct {

    ID     uint   `gorm:"primaryKey"`

    Name   string `gorm:"size:100"`

    Email  string `gorm:"size:100;unique"`

}
```

- `gorm:"primaryKey"`: Marks the field as the primary key.
- `gorm:"size:100"`: Sets the maximum length of the string.
- `gorm:"unique"`: Ensures the field value is unique.

Step 4: Automating Migrations

GORM can automatically create or update tables based on your models using migrations.

go

```go
func main() {

    // Database connection (PostgreSQL example)

    dsn := "user=yourusername password=yourpassword dbname=mydb sslmode=disable"

    db, err := gorm.Open(postgres.Open(dsn), &gorm.Config{})

    if err != nil {

        log.Fatalf("Failed to connect to database: %v", err)
```

```go
    }

    // Automigrate

    err = db.AutoMigrate(&User{})

    if err != nil {

        log.Fatalf("Failed     to     migrate
database: %v", err)

    }

    log.Println("Database           migrated
successfully!")

}
```

Step 5: CRUD Operations with GORM

Create

go

```go
func  createUser(db   *gorm.DB,   name,   email
string) {

    user := User{Name: name, Email: email}

    result := db.Create(&user)

    if result.Error != nil {
```
303

```go
        log.Fatalf("Error   creating   user:
%v", result.Error)

    }

    log.Printf("User created: %+v\n", user)

}
```

Read

```go
func fetchUsers(db *gorm.DB) {

    var users []User

    result := db.Find(&users)

    if result.Error != nil {

        log.Fatalf("Error   fetching   users:
%v", result.Error)

    }

    for _, user := range users {

        log.Printf("User: %+v\n", user)

    }
```

}

Update

go

```go
func updateUserEmail(db *gorm.DB, id uint,
newEmail string) {

    result := db.Model(&User{}).Where("id =
?", id).Update("Email", newEmail)

    if result.Error != nil {

        log.Fatalf("Error   updating   user:
%v", result.Error)

    }

    log.Println("User      email      updated
successfully!")

}
```

Delete

go

```go
func deleteUser(db *gorm.DB, id uint) {
```

```go
    result := db.Delete(&User{}, id)

    if result.Error != nil {

        log.Fatalf("Error    deleting    user:
%v", result.Error)

    }

    log.Println("User                        deleted
successfully!")

}
```

Step 6: Example Program

go

```go
func main() {

    // Connect to the database

    dsn            :=           "user=yourusername
password=yourpassword                dbname=mydb
sslmode=disable"

    db, err := gorm.Open(postgres.Open(dsn),
&gorm.Config{})
```

```go
    if err != nil {

        log.Fatalf("Failed to connect to
database: %v", err)

    }

    // Migrate the schema

    err = db.AutoMigrate(&User{})

    if err != nil {

        log.Fatalf("Failed to migrate
database: %v", err)

    }

    // Perform CRUD operations

    createUser(db, "Alice",
"alice@example.com")

    createUser(db, "Bob", "bob@example.com")

    fetchUsers(db)

    updateUserEmail(db, 1,
"alice.new@example.com")

    deleteUser(db, 2)

}
```

Step 7: Best Practices with GORM

1. **Use Contexts**: Pass a `context.Context` to database operations for better control.
2. **Error Handling**: Always check and handle errors from GORM methods.
3. **Indexing**: Use appropriate indexes for better query performance.
4. **Database Configuration**: Configure database connection pooling and timeouts for production environments.

6.4 Performing CRUD Operations

CRUD (Create, Read, Update, Delete) operations are the backbone of any application that interacts with a database. In this chapter, we'll explore how to perform these operations in Go using both the `database/sql` package and **GORM**. By the end of this chapter, you'll have a solid understanding of how to manage data effectively in your Go applications.

Section 1: CRUD Operations with `database/sql`

Setting Up the Database Connection

Before performing CRUD operations, establish a connection to your database.

go

```go
package main

import (

    "database/sql"

    "fmt"

    "log"


    _   "github.com/lib/pq"   //   PostgreSQL
driver

)

func connectDB() *sql.DB {

    connStr        :=        "user=yourusername
password=yourpassword            dbname=mydb
sslmode=disable"

    db, err := sql.Open("postgres", connStr)

    if err != nil {
```

```go
        log.Fatalf("Failed   to   connect   to
database: %v", err)

    }

    return db

}
```

Create Operation

Insert a new record into the database.

go

```go
func   createUser(db   *sql.DB,   name,   email
string) {

    query := "INSERT INTO users (name, email)
VALUES ($1, $2)"

    _, err := db.Exec(query, name, email)

    if err != nil {

        log.Fatalf("Error   creating   user:
%v", err)

    }
```

```go
    fmt.Println("User                              created
successfully!")

}
```

Read Operation

Fetch records from the database.

go

```go
func fetchUsers(db *sql.DB) {

    query := "SELECT id, name, email FROM
users"

    rows, err := db.Query(query)

    if err != nil {

        log.Fatalf("Error   fetching   users:
%v", err)

    }

    defer rows.Close()


    for rows.Next() {

        var id int
```

```go
        var name, email string

        err = rows.Scan(&id, &name, &email)

        if err != nil {

                log.Fatalf("Error scanning row:
%v", err)

        }

        fmt.Printf("ID: %d, Name: %s, Email:
%s\n", id, name, email)

    }

}
```

Update Operation

Update an existing record.

go

```go
func updateUserEmail(db *sql.DB, id int,
newEmail string) {

    query := "UPDATE users SET email = $1
WHERE id = $2"

    _, err := db.Exec(query, newEmail, id)
```

```go
    if err != nil {

        log.Fatalf("Error    updating    user:
%v", err)

    }

    fmt.Println("User         email       updated
successfully!")

}
```

Delete Operation

Remove a record from the database.

go

```go
func deleteUser(db *sql.DB, id int) {

    query := "DELETE FROM users WHERE id =
$1"

    _, err := db.Exec(query, id)

    if err != nil {

        log.Fatalf("Error    deleting    user:
%v", err)

    }
```

```go
    fmt.Println("User                    deleted
successfully!")

}
```

Full Example with `database/sql`

go

```go
func main() {

    db := connectDB()

    defer db.Close()

    // Create

    createUser(db,                    "Alice",
"alice@example.com")

    // Read

    fetchUsers(db)


    // Update

    updateUserEmail(db,                    1,
"alice.new@example.com")
```

```go
    // Delete

    deleteUser(db, 1)

}
```

Section 2: CRUD Operations with GORM

Create Operation

Insert a new record using GORM.

go

```go
func createUser(db *gorm.DB, name, email
string) {

    user := User{Name: name, Email: email}

    result := db.Create(&user)

    if result.Error != nil {

        log.Fatalf("Error creating user:
%v", result.Error)

    }

    fmt.Printf("User created: %+v\n", user)

}
```

Read Operation

Fetch all records using GORM.

go

```go
func fetchUsers(db *gorm.DB) {

    var users []User

    result := db.Find(&users)

    if result.Error != nil {

        log.Fatalf("Error   fetching   users:
%v", result.Error)

    }

    for _, user := range users {

        fmt.Printf("User: %+v\n", user)

    }

}
```

Update Operation

Update a record using GORM.

go

```go
func updateUserEmail(db *gorm.DB, id uint, newEmail string) {

    result := db.Model(&User{}).Where("id = ?", id).Update("Email", newEmail)

    if result.Error != nil {

        log.Fatalf("Error updating user: %v", result.Error)

    }

    fmt.Println("User email updated successfully!")

}
```

Delete Operation

Delete a record using GORM.

go

```go
func deleteUser(db *gorm.DB, id uint) {

    result := db.Delete(&User{}, id)

    if result.Error != nil {
```

```go
        log.Fatalf("Error    deleting    user:
%v", result.Error)

    }

    fmt.Println("User                    deleted
successfully!")

}
```

Full Example with GORM

go

```go
func main() {

    // Connect to the database

    dsn            :=            "user=yourusername
password=yourpassword              dbname=mydb
sslmode=disable"

    db, err := gorm.Open(postgres.Open(dsn),
&gorm.Config{})

    if err != nil {

        log.Fatalf("Failed   to   connect   to
database: %v", err)

    }
```

```go
    // Migrate the schema

    err = db.AutoMigrate(&User{})

    if err != nil {

        log.Fatalf("Failed     to     migrate
database: %v", err)

    }


    // Perform CRUD operations

    createUser(db, "Bob", "bob@example.com")

    fetchUsers(db)

    updateUserEmail(db,                      1,
"bob.new@example.com")

    deleteUser(db, 1)

}
```

Hands-On Project: Build a Go application that connects to a database to manage a list of products.

This project will guide you through building a Go application that connects to a database to manage a list of products. The application will allow users to perform CRUD operations (Create, Read, Update, Delete). By the end of this chapter, you will have a fully functional application and a strong understanding of database interactions using Go and GORM.

Step 1: Setting Up the Environment

Prerequisites

Ensure you have the following installed:

1. **Go**: Install Go.
2. **PostgreSQL**: Install and set up PostgreSQL (or use MySQL if preferred).
3. **GORM**: Install GORM and the PostgreSQL driver.

Install the necessary Go packages:

bash

```
go get -u gorm.io/gorm

go get -u gorm.io/driver/postgres
```

Step 2: Designing the Database

Create the Database and Table

Set up a PostgreSQL database named product_manager and create a products table.

Run the following SQL commands:

sql

```sql
CREATE DATABASE product_manager;

\c product_manager

CREATE TABLE products (

    id SERIAL PRIMARY KEY,

    name VARCHAR(100) NOT NULL,

    description TEXT,

    price NUMERIC(10, 2) NOT NULL,

    stock INT NOT NULL

);
```

Step 3: Setting Up the Project

Initialize the Project

Create a new directory for your project and initialize a Go module:

bash

```
mkdir product-manager

cd product-manager

go mod init product-manager
```

Directory Structure

Organize your project files as follows:

go

```
product-manager/

├── main.go

├── database/

│   └── connection.go

├── models/

│   └── product.go
```

```
├── handlers/

│   └── product_handler.go
```

Step 4: Connecting to the Database

File: `database/connection.go`

This file will handle the database connection using GORM.

go

```go
package database

import (

    "gorm.io/driver/postgres"

    "gorm.io/gorm"

    "log"

)

var DB *gorm.DB

func ConnectDatabase() {
```

```go
    dsn := "host=localhost user=your_user
password=your_password
dbname=product_manager           port=5432
sslmode=disable"

    database,            err            :=
gorm.Open(postgres.Open(dsn),
&gorm.Config{})

    if err != nil {

        log.Fatal("Failed to connect to the
database:", err)

    }


    DB = database

    log.Println("Database           connection
established successfully.")

}
```

Step 5: Defining the Product Model

File: `models/product.go`

This file defines the `Product` struct that maps to the `products` table.

go

```
package models

type Product struct {

    ID          uint    `gorm:"primaryKey"`

    Name          string `gorm:"size:100;not
null"`

    Description string

    Price       float64 `gorm:"not null"`

    Stock       int     `gorm:"not null"`

}
```

Step 6: Writing Handlers for CRUD Operations

File: `handlers/product_handler.go`

This file contains the logic for handling CRUD operations.

go

```
package handlers
```

```go
import (

    "encoding/json"

    "net/http"

    "product-manager/database"

    "product-manager/models"

    "strconv"

    "github.com/gorilla/mux"

)

func GetProducts(w http.ResponseWriter, r
*http.Request) {

    var products []models.Product

    database.DB.Find(&products)

    w.Header().Set("Content-Type",
"application/json")

    json.NewEncoder(w).Encode(products)

}

func GetProductByID(w http.ResponseWriter, r
*http.Request) {

    params := mux.Vars(r)
```

```go
    id, _ := strconv.Atoi(params["id"])

    var product models.Product

    if err := database.DB.First(&product,
id).Error; err != nil {

        http.Error(w, "Product not found",
http.StatusNotFound)

        return

    }

    w.Header().Set("Content-Type",
"application/json")

    json.NewEncoder(w).Encode(product)

}

func CreateProduct(w http.ResponseWriter, r
*http.Request) {

    var product models.Product

    json.NewDecoder(r.Body).Decode(&product
)

    database.DB.Create(&product)

    w.Header().Set("Content-Type",
"application/json")
```

```go
    json.NewEncoder(w).Encode(product)

}


func UpdateProduct(w http.ResponseWriter, r
*http.Request) {

    params := mux.Vars(r)

    id, _ := strconv.Atoi(params["id"])


    var product models.Product

    if err := database.DB.First(&product,
id).Error; err != nil {

        http.Error(w, "Product not found",
http.StatusNotFound)

        return

    }


    json.NewDecoder(r.Body).Decode(&product
)

    database.DB.Save(&product)
```

```go
    w.Header().Set("Content-Type",
"application/json")

    json.NewEncoder(w).Encode(product)

}

func DeleteProduct(w http.ResponseWriter, r
*http.Request) {

    params := mux.Vars(r)

    id, _ := strconv.Atoi(params["id"])

    var product models.Product

    if err := database.DB.First(&product,
id).Error; err != nil {

        http.Error(w, "Product not found",
http.StatusNotFound)

        return

    }


    database.DB.Delete(&product)

    w.WriteHeader(http.StatusNoContent)

}
```

Step 7: Setting Up the Main Application

File: `main.go`

This file sets up the application, routes, and starts the server.

go

```go
package main

import (

    "log"

    "net/http"

    "product-manager/database"

    "product-manager/handlers"


    "github.com/gorilla/mux"
)


func main() {

    // Connect to the database
```

```go
    database.ConnectDatabase()


    // Migrate the database
    database.DB.AutoMigrate(&models.Product
{})


    // Set up the router
    r := mux.NewRouter()


    // Define routes
    r.HandleFunc("/products",
handlers.GetProducts).Methods("GET")

    r.HandleFunc("/products/{id}",
handlers.GetProductByID).Methods("GET")

    r.HandleFunc("/products",
handlers.CreateProduct).Methods("POST")

    r.HandleFunc("/products/{id}",
handlers.UpdateProduct).Methods("PUT")

    r.HandleFunc("/products/{id}",
handlers.DeleteProduct).Methods("DELETE")
```

```go
    // Start the server

    log.Println("Server is running on port
8080")

    log.Fatal(http.ListenAndServe(":8080",
r))

}
```

Step 8: Testing the Application

Run the Application
Start the server:
bash

```bash
go run main.go
```

1. **Test with Postman or Curl**
   - **GET** /products: Fetch all products.
   - **POST** /products: Add a new product.
   - **GET** /products/{id}: Fetch a product by ID.
   - **PUT** /products/{id}: Update a product.
   - **DELETE** /products/{id}: Delete a product.

Chapter 7: Authentication and Authorization

Authentication and authorization are critical components of modern web applications. Authentication ensures that users are who they claim to be, while authorization determines what authenticated users can do. In this chapter, we will explore how to implement these concepts in Go using JWT (JSON Web Tokens), integrate OAuth for social logins, and enforce role-based access control (RBAC).

7.1 Implementing User Authentication with JWT

User authentication is a critical part of modern web applications. It ensures that only authorized users can access specific resources. One popular method for implementing authentication in web applications is by using **JSON Web Tokens (JWT)**. This chapter will guide you through the fundamentals of JWT, its structure, and how to implement it in a Go application.

What is JWT?

JSON Web Token (JWT) is a compact and self-contained token format for securely transmitting information between parties as a JSON object. It is widely used for authentication and information exchange due to its simplicity and flexibility.

Structure of a JWT

A JWT is composed of three parts:

1. **Header**: Contains metadata about the token, such as the type of token and the hashing algorithm used.
2. **Payload**: Includes claims, which are statements about the user or additional data.
3. **Signature**: Ensures the token's integrity and authenticity.

Example JWT:

```
eyJhbGciOiJIUzI1NiIsInR5cCI6IkpXVCJ9.eyJ1c2V
ySWQiOjEsInJvbGUiOiJ1c2VyIn0.abc123signature
```

- **Header**: `{"alg": "HS256", "typ": "JWT"}`
- **Payload**: `{"userId": 1, "role": "user"}`
- **Signature**: Created using a secret key and the header + payload.

How JWT Works

1. **User Login**: The user sends their credentials (e.g., username and password).
2. **Token Issuance**: The server validates the credentials and issues a JWT.

3. **Client Storage**: The client stores the JWT (e.g., in localStorage or a cookie).
4. **Token Validation**: The client includes the JWT in the Authorization header of subsequent requests. The server validates the token before processing the request.

Step-by-Step Implementation in Go

Step 1: Install the Required Package

To work with JWTs in Go, install the `github.com/golang-jwt/jwt/v5` package:

bash

```
go get -u github.com/golang-jwt/jwt/v5
```

Step 2: Define the JWT Utility Functions

Create a utility file to handle JWT creation and validation.

File: `utils/jwt.go`

go

```
package utils

import (
```

```go
    "time"

    "github.com/golang-jwt/jwt/v5"
)


var jwtKey = []byte("your_secret_key") // Replace with a secure secret key


type Claims struct {
    UserID uint   `json:"userId"`
    Role   string `json:"role"`
    jwt.RegisteredClaims
}


// GenerateJWT generates a new JWT for a user
func GenerateJWT(userID uint, role string) (string, error) {
    claims := &Claims{
```

```go
        UserID: userID,

        Role:    role,

        RegisteredClaims:
jwt.RegisteredClaims{

            ExpiresAt:
jwt.NewNumericDate(time.Now().Add(24        *
time.Hour)), // Token valid for 24 hours

        },

    }


    token                              :=
jwt.NewWithClaims(jwt.SigningMethodHS256,
claims)

    return token.SignedString(jwtKey)

}


// ValidateJWT validates a JWT and extracts
claims

func ValidateJWT(tokenStr string) (*Claims,
error) {
```

```go
    claims := &Claims{}

    token, err :=
jwt.ParseWithClaims(tokenStr, claims,
func(token *jwt.Token) (interface{}, error) {

        return jwtKey, nil

    })


    if err != nil || !token.Valid {

        return nil, err

    }


    return claims, nil

}
```

Step 3: Implement User Login Endpoint

Create an endpoint to authenticate users and issue JWTs.

File: `handlers/auth.go`

```go
package handlers

import (

    "encoding/json"

    "net/http"

    "yourapp/models"

    "yourapp/utils"


    "gorm.io/gorm"
)


func Login(w http.ResponseWriter, r
*http.Request) {

    var credentials struct {

        Email    string `json:"email"`

        Password string `json:"password"`

    }
```

```go
    // Parse the JSON request body

    if            err            :=
json.NewDecoder(r.Body).Decode(&credentials)
; err != nil {

        http.Error(w,  "Invalid  request",
http.StatusBadRequest)

        return

    }


    // Check user credentials in the database

    var user models.User

    if err := database.DB.Where("email = ?",
credentials.Email).First(&user).Error;   err
!= nil {

        if err == gorm.ErrRecordNotFound {

        http.Error(w,              "Invalid
credentials", http.StatusUnauthorized)

        return

        }
```

```go
        http.Error(w,    "Internal    server
error", http.StatusInternalServerError)

        return

    }


    // Verify password (use hashed passwords
in production)

    if user.Password != credentials.Password
{

        http.Error(w, "Invalid credentials",
http.StatusUnauthorized)

        return

    }


    // Generate JWT

    token, err := utils.GenerateJWT(user.ID,
user.Role)

    if err != nil {

        http.Error(w,    "Internal    server
error", http.StatusInternalServerError)
```

```go
        return
    }


    // Return the token
    w.Header().Set("Content-Type",
"application/json")

    json.NewEncoder(w).Encode(map[string]st
ring{"token": token})
}
```

Step 4: Protect Routes with JWT Middleware

Create middleware to validate JWTs for protected routes.

File: `middleware/auth.go`

go

```go
package middleware

import (

    "net/http"

    "strings"
```

```go
    "yourapp/utils"
)

func JWTAuth(next http.Handler) http.Handler
{

    return            http.HandlerFunc(func(w
http.ResponseWriter, r *http.Request) {

        authHeader                    :=
r.Header.Get("Authorization")

        if authHeader == "" {

            http.Error(w,    "Unauthorized",
http.StatusUnauthorized)

            return

        }



        tokenStr                      :=
strings.TrimPrefix(authHeader, "Bearer ")

        claims,        err            :=
utils.ValidateJWT(tokenStr)

        if err != nil {
```

```go
            http.Error(w,  "Invalid  token",
http.StatusUnauthorized)

            return

        }

        // Add claims to the request context

        ctx                              :=
context.WithValue(r.Context(),        "user",
claims)

        next.ServeHTTP(w,
r.WithContext(ctx))

    })

}
```

Step 5: Apply Middleware to Routes

Protect routes using the JWT middleware.

File: `main.go`

go

```go
package main

import (
```

```go
    "net/http"

    "yourapp/handlers"

    "yourapp/middleware"


    "github.com/gorilla/mux"
)


func main() {
    r := mux.NewRouter()


    // Public routes
    r.HandleFunc("/login",
handlers.Login).Methods("POST")


    // Protected routes
    protected                              :=
r.PathPrefix("/api").Subrouter()

    protected.Use(middleware.JWTAuth)
```

```
protected.HandleFunc("/products",
handlers.GetProducts).Methods("GET")


    http.ListenAndServe(":8080", r)

}
```

Testing the Implementation

1. **Login**: Send a POST request to `/login` with valid credentials. The response will include a JWT.
2. **Access Protected Routes**: Include the JWT in the `Authorization` header (`Bearer <token>`) when accessing protected routes.

Real-World Considerations

- **Secure Storage**: Store the JWT securely on the client side (e.g., HttpOnly cookies).
- **Token Expiry**: Handle token expiration gracefully by implementing refresh tokens.
- **Password Security**: Always hash passwords using a secure hashing algorithm like bcrypt.

7.2 OAuth Integration for Social Logins

Social logins have become a common feature in modern web applications, providing users with a convenient way to authenticate using their existing accounts from platforms like Google, Facebook, or GitHub. This chapter will guide you through integrating OAuth 2.0 for social logins in a Go application, using Google as an example.

What is OAuth 2.0?

OAuth 2.0 is an open standard for access delegation. It allows third-party applications to access user resources without exposing user credentials. OAuth 2.0 is widely used for social logins, enabling users to log in to your application using their existing accounts.

How OAuth 2.0 Works

1. **User Request**: The user clicks a "Login with Google" button.
2. **Authorization Code**: The user is redirected to the provider (e.g., Google) to grant permission.
3. **Access Token**: The provider returns an authorization code to your application, which exchanges it for an access token.
4. **User Data**: Your application uses the access token to fetch user data from the provider.

5. **Login/Signup**: Based on the user data, you log in the user or create a new account.

Step-by-Step Implementation in Go

Step 1: Install Required Packages

Install the `golang.org/x/oauth2` package for OAuth 2.0 and `golang.org/x/oauth2/google` for Google integration:

bash

```
go get golang.org/x/oauth2

go get golang.org/x/oauth2/google
```

Step 2: Create OAuth Configuration

Define the OAuth 2.0 configuration for Google.

File: `config/oauth.go`

go

```
package config

import (

    "golang.org/x/oauth2"
```

```go
    "golang.org/x/oauth2/google"

)


var GoogleOAuthConfig = &oauth2.Config{

    ClientID:        "your_google_client_id",
// Replace with your Google Client ID

    ClientSecret:
"your_google_client_secret", // Replace with
your Google Client Secret

    RedirectURL:
"http://localhost:8080/auth/google/callback"
,

    Scopes:
[]string{"https://www.googleapis.com/auth/us
erinfo.email",
"https://www.googleapis.com/auth/userinfo.pr
ofile"},

    Endpoint:        google.Endpoint,

}
```

Step 3: Create the Login Handler

The login handler redirects users to Google's OAuth 2.0 endpoint.

File: `handlers/auth.go`

go

```go
package handlers

import (

    "net/http"

    "yourapp/config"

)



func GoogleLogin(w http.ResponseWriter, r *http.Request) {

    url := config.GoogleOAuthConfig.AuthCodeURL("state-token", oauth2.AccessTypeOffline)

    http.Redirect(w, r, url, http.StatusTemporaryRedirect)

}
```

Step 4: Handle the Callback

Once the user grants permission, Google redirects them back to your application with an authorization code. Exchange this code for an access token and fetch user information.

File: `handlers/auth.go`

```go
package handlers

import (

    "encoding/json"

    "fmt"

    "io/ioutil"

    "net/http"

    "yourapp/config"


    "golang.org/x/oauth2"

)
```

```go
func GoogleCallback(w http.ResponseWriter, r
*http.Request) {

    // Get the authorization code from the
query parameters

    code := r.URL.Query().Get("code")

    if code == "" {

        http.Error(w,  "Authorization  code
not found", http.StatusBadRequest)

        return

    }


    // Exchange the authorization code for an
access token

    token,              err              :=
config.GoogleOAuthConfig.Exchange(oauth2.NoC
ontext, code)

    if err != nil {

        http.Error(w,  "Failed  to  exchange
token", http.StatusInternalServerError)

        return
```

```go
    }

    // Fetch user information

    client :=
config.GoogleOAuthConfig.Client(oauth2.NoCon
text, token)

    resp, err :=
client.Get("https://www.googleapis.com/oauth
2/v2/userinfo")

    if err != nil {

        http.Error(w, "Failed to fetch user
info", http.StatusInternalServerError)

        return

    }

    defer resp.Body.Close()


    // Parse the user information

    body, err := ioutil.ReadAll(resp.Body)

    if err != nil {
```

```go
        http.Error(w,  "Failed   to   read
response                      body",
http.StatusInternalServerError)

        return

    }


    var userInfo map[string]interface{}

    if    err    :=    json.Unmarshal(body,
&userInfo); err != nil {

        http.Error(w, "Failed to parse user
info", http.StatusInternalServerError)

        return

    }


    // Print or process the user information

    fmt.Fprintf(w,   "User    Info:    %v",
userInfo)

}
```

Step 5: Add Routes for Social Login

Define routes for the login and callback handlers.

File: `main.go`

```go
package main

import (

    "net/http"

    "yourapp/handlers"


    "github.com/gorilla/mux"
)

func main() {

    r := mux.NewRouter()


    // Google OAuth routes

    r.HandleFunc("/auth/google/login",
handlers.GoogleLogin).Methods("GET")
```

```
    r.HandleFunc("/auth/google/callback",
handlers.GoogleCallback).Methods("GET")


    http.ListenAndServe(":8080", r)

}
```

Step 6: Testing the Integration

1. **Set Up a Google API Project:**
   - Go to the Google Cloud Console.
   - Create a new project and enable the "Google+ API".
   - Generate OAuth 2.0 credentials (Client ID and Client Secret).
   - Set the redirect URI to
     `http://localhost:8080/auth/google/callback`.

2. **Start the Application**:
   - Run your Go application: `go run main.go`.
   - Open
     `http://localhost:8080/auth/google/login` in your browser.
   - Log in with your Google account.

3. **Verify User Information**:
   - After successful login, Google redirects you to the callback endpoint.

○ Your application prints the user information.

Real-World Considerations

- **State Parameter**: Use the `state` parameter to prevent CSRF attacks during the OAuth flow.
- **Secure Storage**: Store access tokens securely (e.g., encrypted database storage).
- **Refresh Tokens**: Handle token expiration by using refresh tokens.
- **Multiple Providers**: Extend the implementation to support other providers like Facebook, GitHub, etc.

7.3 Role-Based Access Control in Go

Role-Based Access Control (RBAC) is a method of managing user permissions based on roles assigned to users. It simplifies permission management by grouping permissions into roles and assigning these roles to users. This chapter will guide you through implementing RBAC in a Go application, ensuring secure and efficient user access control.

What is Role-Based Access Control?

RBAC assigns permissions to roles rather than individual users. For example:

- **Admin Role**: Can manage users, products, and orders.
- **User Role**: Can view and purchase products.
- **Guest Role**: Can only view products.

With RBAC, you can:

1. **Define Roles**: Create roles with specific permissions.
2. **Assign Roles**: Assign one or more roles to users.
3. **Check Permissions**: Verify if a user has the required role to access a resource.

Step-by-Step Implementation in Go

Step 1: Define Roles and Permissions

Create a structure to define roles and their associated permissions.

File: `models/roles.go`

go

```go
package models

// Role defines a user role with associated
permissions
```

```go
type Role struct {

    Name        string

    Permissions []string

}

// Predefined roles

var (

    AdminRole = Role{

        Name:           "admin",

        Permissions:
[]string{"manage_users",  "manage_products",
"view_orders"},

    }

    UserRole = Role{

        Name:           "user",

        Permissions:
[]string{"view_products", "place_order"},

    }

    GuestRole = Role{

        Name:           "guest",
```

```go
        Permissions:
[]string{"view_products"},

    }

)

// Map roles for quick access

var Roles = map[string]Role{

    "admin": AdminRole,

    "user":  UserRole,

    "guest": GuestRole,

}
```

Step 2: Assign Roles to Users

Simulate user-role assignments using a simple data structure.

File: `models/users.go`

go

```go
package models

// User defines a user with roles

type User struct {
```

```go
    ID    int

    Name  string

    Email string

    Roles []string

}

// Sample users

var Users = []User{

    {ID:    1,    Name:    "Alice",    Email:
"alice@example.com",                    Roles:
[]string{"admin"}},

    {ID:    2,    Name:    "Bob",    Email:
"bob@example.com", Roles: []string{"user"}},

    {ID:    3,    Name:    "Charlie",    Email:
"charlie@example.com",                  Roles:
[]string{"guest"}},

}
```

Step 3: Middleware for Role Verification

Create middleware to check if a user has the required role for accessing
a route.

File: `middleware/role_middleware.go`

go

```
package middleware

import (

    "net/http"

    "strings"

    "yourapp/models"

)

// CheckRoleMiddleware verifies if a user has
the required role

func        CheckRoleMiddleware(requiredRole
string,        next        http.HandlerFunc)
http.HandlerFunc {

    return  func(w  http.ResponseWriter,  r
*http.Request) {

        // Simulate fetching the user (e.g.,
from a session or JWT)

        userEmail  :=  r.Header.Get("X-User-
Email")

        var user *models.User
```

```go
    for _, u := range models.Users {
        if   strings.EqualFold(u.Email,
userEmail) {
            user = &u
            break
        }
    }


    if user == nil {
        http.Error(w, "User not found",
http.StatusUnauthorized)
        return
    }
    // Check if the user has the required
role
    for _, role := range user.Roles {
        if role == requiredRole {
            next(w, r)
            return
```

```go
        }

      }

      http.Error(w,    "Access    denied",
http.StatusForbidden)

    }

}
```

Step 4: Protect Routes with Role-Based Middleware

Apply the middleware to specific routes based on the required roles.

File: main.go

go

```go
package main

import (

    "fmt"

    "net/http"

    "yourapp/middleware"


    "github.com/gorilla/mux"
```

```go
)

func main() {

    r := mux.NewRouter()


    // Public route

    r.HandleFunc("/products",            func(w
http.ResponseWriter, r *http.Request) {

        fmt.Fprintln(w, "All Products")

    }).Methods("GET")

    // Protected route for "user" role

    r.HandleFunc("/orders",
middleware.CheckRoleMiddleware("user",
func(w http.ResponseWriter, r *http.Request)
{

        fmt.Fprintln(w, "Your Orders")

    })).Methods("GET")

    // Protected route for "admin" role

    r.HandleFunc("/admin",
middleware.CheckRoleMiddleware("admin",
```

```go
func(w http.ResponseWriter, r *http.Request)
{

        fmt.Fprintln(w, "Admin Dashboard")

    })).Methods("GET")


    http.ListenAndServe(":8080", r)

}
```

Step 5: Testing the Application

1. **Start the Server:**
   - Run the application: `go run main.go`.
2. **Simulate User Requests**:
   - Use a tool like `curl` or Postman to send requests.
   - Include the `X-User-Email` header to simulate user authentication.

Example Requests:

bash

```bash
# Guest accessing products

curl -H "X-User-Email: charlie@example.com"
http://localhost:8080/products
```

```
# User accessing orders

curl  -H  "X-User-Email:  bob@example.com"
http://localhost:8080/orders

# Guest attempting to access admin dashboard

curl -H "X-User-Email: charlie@example.com"
http://localhost:8080/admin
```

Real-World Considerations

1. **Dynamic Role Management**:
   - Store roles and permissions in a database for easier management.
   - Create an admin panel for modifying roles dynamically.
2. **Multiple Roles**:
   - Allow users to have multiple roles and check for cumulative permissions.
3. **JWT Integration**:
   - Include user roles in JWT claims to avoid fetching roles from the database on every request.
4. **Audit Logs**:
   - Log access attempts to track unauthorized actions.

7.4 Securing Sensitive Endpoints

Securing sensitive endpoints is a critical aspect of building a secure web application. Sensitive endpoints are routes that provide access to confidential information or critical operations, such as managing user accounts, processing payments, or accessing private data. In this chapter, we will explore strategies to secure these endpoints effectively.

Understanding Sensitive Endpoints

Sensitive endpoints often include:

- **Admin Dashboards**: Access to application-wide settings.
- **User Data Management**: CRUD operations on user data.
- **Payment Processing**: Handling financial transactions.
- **Private APIs**: Endpoints not intended for public use.

Failure to secure these endpoints can lead to data breaches, unauthorized access, and system compromise.

Strategies for Securing Sensitive Endpoints

1. Authentication

Authentication ensures that only authorized users can access the application. Use robust authentication mechanisms such as:

- **JWT (JSON Web Tokens)** for stateless authentication.
- **OAuth** for third-party login systems.
- **Session-based Authentication** for traditional web apps.

Example: Middleware to enforce authentication.

File: `middleware/auth.go`

go

```
package middleware

import (

    "net/http"

)

// AuthMiddleware verifies if the user is
authenticated

func AuthMiddleware(next http.HandlerFunc)
http.HandlerFunc {

    return func(w http.ResponseWriter, r
*http.Request) {

        token                           :=
r.Header.Get("Authorization")

        if token == "" {
```

```
            http.Error(w,    "Unauthorized",
http.StatusUnauthorized)

            return

        }

        // Validate token (pseudo-code,
replace with actual logic)

        if !validateToken(token) {

            http.Error(w, "Invalid token",
http.StatusUnauthorized)

            return

        }

        next(w, r)

    }

}

// Dummy token validation function

func validateToken(token string) bool {

    return token == "valid-token"

}
```

2. Authorization

Authorization ensures that authenticated users have the appropriate permissions to access a resource. Implement Role-Based Access Control (RBAC) or Attribute-Based Access Control (ABAC) for granular permission management.

Example: Middleware to check permissions.

File: `middleware/authorization.go`

go

```go
package middleware

import (

    "net/http"

)

// PermissionMiddleware verifies if the user
has the required permission

func PermissionMiddleware(requiredPermission
string,        next        http.HandlerFunc)
http.HandlerFunc {

    return  func(w  http.ResponseWriter,  r
*http.Request) {
```

```
        // Simulate fetching user
permissions

        userPermissions            :=
[]string{"view_products", "place_order"}


        // Check if the user has the required
permission

        for _, perm := range userPermissions
{

                if perm == requiredPermission {

                        next(w, r)

                        return

                }

        }


        http.Error(w,              "Forbidden",
http.StatusForbidden)

    }

}
```

3. Rate Limiting

Rate limiting prevents abuse of sensitive endpoints by limiting the number of requests a user or IP address can make in a given time.

Example: Simple rate limiting using an in-memory counter.

File: `middleware/rate_limiter.go`

go

```go
package middleware

import (

    "net/http"

    "sync"

    "time"

)

var (

    requests = make(map[string]int)

    mu        sync.Mutex

)
```

```go
// RateLimiter limits requests to a certain
threshold

func      RateLimiter(limit      int,      next
http.HandlerFunc) http.HandlerFunc {

    return   func(w   http.ResponseWriter,   r
*http.Request) {

        ip := r.RemoteAddr

        mu.Lock()

        defer mu.Unlock()


        // Increment request count

        requests[ip]++

        if requests[ip] > limit {

            http.Error(w,       "Too       many
requests", http.StatusTooManyRequests)

            return

        }


        // Reset count after a minute
```

```go
    go func() {

        time.Sleep(time.Minute)

        mu.Lock()

        requests[ip]--

        mu.Unlock()

    }()


    next(w, r)

    }

}
```

4. Input Validation

Validate all user inputs to prevent injection attacks (e.g., SQL injection, XSS). Use libraries like `sqlx` or ORM frameworks like GORM to handle input safely.

Example: Validating user input.

```go
package main

import (

    "encoding/json"

    "net/http"

    "regexp"

)

type Input struct {

    Username string `json:"username"`

    Email    string `json:"email"`

}

func validateInput(input Input) error {

    // Validate username (alphanumeric, 3-20 characters)

    if matched, _ := regexp.MatchString("^[a-zA-Z0-9]{3,20}$", input.Username); !matched {

        return fmt.Errorf("invalid username")
```

```go
    }


    // Validate email

    if        matched,        _        :=
regexp.MatchString(`^[a-z0-9._%+-]+@[a-z0-
9.-]+\.[a-z]{2,4}$`, input.Email); !matched {

        return fmt.Errorf("invalid email")

    }


    return nil
}
func    handler(w    http.ResponseWriter,    r
*http.Request) {

    var input Input

    if                err                :=
json.NewDecoder(r.Body).Decode(&input);    err
!= nil {

        http.Error(w,    "Invalid    input",
http.StatusBadRequest)

        return
```

```go
    }

    if err := validateInput(input); err !=
nil {

        http.Error(w,               err.Error(),
http.StatusBadRequest)

        return

    }

    w.WriteHeader(http.StatusOK)

    w.Write([]byte("Input is valid"))

}
```

5. HTTPS

Always use HTTPS to encrypt data in transit, protecting sensitive information from being intercepted.

6. Audit Logging

Log all access attempts to sensitive endpoints, including:

- **User ID** or IP address.
- **Timestamp**.

- **Endpoint accessed.**

Use these logs for monitoring and forensic analysis.

Putting It All Together

File: `main.go`

go

```
package main

import (

    "fmt"

    "net/http"

    "yourapp/middleware"

    "github.com/gorilla/mux"

)

func main() {

    r := mux.NewRouter()

    // Public route

    r.HandleFunc("/public",            func(w
http.ResponseWriter, r *http.Request) {
```

```go
        fmt.Fprintln(w, "Public Endpoint")

    }).Methods("GET")


    // Secured route with authentication

    r.HandleFunc("/secure",
middleware.AuthMiddleware(func(w
http.ResponseWriter, r *http.Request) {

        fmt.Fprintln(w, "Secure Endpoint")

    })).Methods("GET")


    // Admin route with authentication and
authorization

    r.HandleFunc("/admin",
middleware.AuthMiddleware(


    middleware.PermissionMiddleware("manage
_users",   func(w   http.ResponseWriter,   r
*http.Request) {

            fmt.Fprintln(w,            "Admin
Dashboard")
```

```
        }),

    )).Methods("GET")


    http.ListenAndServe(":8080", r)

}
```

Testing the Application

1. **Start the Server**:
    - Run the application: `go run main.go`.
2. **Test Endpoints**:
    - Use Postman or `curl` to simulate requests.
    - Include authentication headers for secured routes.

Hands-On Project: Add user authentication to the task management application built earlier.

In this hands-on project, we will enhance the task management application built earlier by adding user authentication. The goal is to ensure that only registered users can access their tasks, and to provide a secure mechanism for login and registration.

Objectives

1. **Implement user registration and login functionality**.
2. **Use JWT (JSON Web Tokens) for secure and stateless authentication**.
3. **Protect task management endpoints to ensure only authenticated users can access them**.

Step 1: Setup the Project

1.1 Initialize the Project

Ensure you have the task management application set up. If not, initialize a new project:

bash

```
mkdir task-manager-auth

cd task-manager-auth

go mod init task-manager-auth
```

1.2 Install Dependencies

Install the necessary libraries:

bash

```bash
go get github.com/gorilla/mux

go get github.com/dgrijalva/jwt-go

go get github.com/jinzhu/gorm

go get github.com/mattn/go-sqlite3
```

Step 2: Database Setup

2.1 Create the User Model

Add a User struct to represent users in the database.

File: models/user.go

go

```go
package models

import "gorm.io/gorm"

type User struct {

    gorm.Model

    Username      string      `gorm:"unique" json:"username"`

    Password string `json:"password"`
```

}

2.2 Update Database Initialization

Update the database initialization to include the User model.

File: `main.go`

go

```
package main

import (

    "log"

    "task-manager-auth/models"

    "gorm.io/driver/sqlite"

    "gorm.io/gorm"

)

var DB *gorm.DB

func initDatabase() {

    var err error
```

```go
    DB,                    err                    =
gorm.Open(sqlite.Open("tasks.db"),
&gorm.Config{})

    if err != nil {

        log.Fatal("Failed    to    connect    to
database:", err)

    }


    DB.AutoMigrate(&models.User{})

    log.Println("Database    connected    and
migrated")

}

func main() {

    initDatabase()

    // Additional setup will go here

}
```

Step 3: Implement JWT Authentication

3.1 Create a Utility for JWT

File: `utils/jwt.go`

go

```go
package utils

import (

    "time"

    "github.com/dgrijalva/jwt-go"

)


var jwtKey = []byte("your_secret_key")


type Claims struct {

    Username string `json:"username"`

    jwt.StandardClaims

}

func GenerateJWT(username string) (string,
error) {

    expirationTime := time.Now().Add(24 *
time.Hour)
```

```go
    claims := &Claims{

        Username: username,

        StandardClaims: jwt.StandardClaims{

            ExpiresAt:
expirationTime.Unix(),

            },

    }

    token :=
jwt.NewWithClaims(jwt.SigningMethodHS256,
claims)

    return token.SignedString(jwtKey)

}

func ValidateJWT(tokenStr string) (*Claims,
error) {

    claims := &Claims{}

    token, err :=
jwt.ParseWithClaims(tokenStr, claims,
func(token *jwt.Token) (interface{}, error)
{

        return jwtKey, nil
```

```go
    })
    if err != nil || !token.Valid {
        return nil, err
    }
    return claims, nil
}
```

Step 4: User Registration and Login

4.1 Registration Handler

File: **handlers/auth.go**

go

```go
package handlers

import (
    "encoding/json"
    "net/http"
    "task-manager-auth/models"
    "golang.org/x/crypto/bcrypt"
```

```
    "task-manager-auth/main"

)

func    Register(w    http.ResponseWriter,    r
*http.Request) {

    var user models.User

    json.NewDecoder(r.Body).Decode(&user)

    hashedPassword,            err            :=
bcrypt.GenerateFromPassword([]byte(user.Pass
word), bcrypt.DefaultCost)

    if err != nil {

        http.Error(w,    "Failed    to    hash
password", http.StatusInternalServerError)

        return

    }

    user.Password = string(hashedPassword)

    if err := main.DB.Create(&user).Error;
err != nil {

        http.Error(w,   "Failed    to    create
user", http.StatusInternalServerError)

        return
```

```go
    }

    w.WriteHeader(http.StatusCreated)

    w.Write([]byte("User            registered
successfully"))

}
```

4.2 Login Handler

File: `handlers/auth.go`

go

```go
func    Login(w      http.ResponseWriter,     r
*http.Request) {

    var user models.User

    var input models.User

    json.NewDecoder(r.Body).Decode(&input)


    if err := main.DB.Where("username = ?",
input.Username).First(&user).Error;  err  !=
nil {

        http.Error(w,  "Invalid  username  or
password", http.StatusUnauthorized)
```

```go
        return

    }

    if                    err                    :=
bcrypt.CompareHashAndPassword([]byte(user.Pa
ssword), []byte(input.Password)); err != nil
{

        http.Error(w,  "Invalid  username  or
password", http.StatusUnauthorized)

        return

    }

    token,                 err                :=
utils.GenerateJWT(user.Username)

    if err != nil {

        http.Error(w,  "Failed  to  generate
token", http.StatusInternalServerError)

        return

    }

    w.Write([]byte(token))

}
```

Step 5: Protect Task Endpoints

5.1 Middleware for Authentication

File: `middleware/auth.go`

go

```go
package middleware

import (

    "net/http"

    "strings"

    "task-manager-auth/utils"

)

func AuthMiddleware(next http.HandlerFunc)
http.HandlerFunc {

    return func(w http.ResponseWriter, r
*http.Request) {

        token                          :=
strings.TrimSpace(r.Header.Get("Authorizatio
n"))

        if token == "" {
```

```go
            http.Error(w,      "Unauthorized",
http.StatusUnauthorized)

        return

    }

    _, err := utils.ValidateJWT(token)

    if err != nil {

        http.Error(w,  "Invalid  token",
http.StatusUnauthorized)

        return

    }

    next(w, r)

  }

}
```

5.2 Protect Task Routes

Update your task routes to include the middleware.

File: `main.go`

go

```
r.HandleFunc("/tasks",
middleware.AuthMiddleware(handlers.GetTasks)
).Methods("GET")

r.HandleFunc("/tasks",
middleware.AuthMiddleware(handlers.CreateTas
k)).Methods("POST")
```

Step 6: Test the Application

Run the Server:

bash

```
go run main.go
```

1. **Register a User**: Use Postman or `curl` to send a POST request to `/register`.
2. **Login**: Send a POST request to `/login` and retrieve the token.
3. **Access Protected Endpoints**: Include the token in the `Authorization` header to access `/tasks`.

Chapter 8: Real-Time Web Applications with Websockets

Real-time web applications are increasingly popular for delivering interactive user experiences. Websockets are a key technology for building such applications, enabling full-duplex communication between the client and server over a single TCP connection. In this chapter, we'll dive into Websockets and use them to build a real-time chat application in Go.

8.1 Introduction to Websockets and Real-Time Features

The demand for real-time web applications has grown significantly, driven by the need for interactive, responsive user experiences. From chat applications and live notifications to collaborative tools and online gaming, real-time communication is at the heart of modern web development. In this chapter, we'll explore Websockets, a key technology that enables real-time communication, and lay the foundation for building real-time applications in Go.

What Are Websockets?

Websockets are a protocol that provides full-duplex communication channels over a single TCP connection. Unlike traditional HTTP, which operates in a request-response cycle, Websockets allow the server and client to exchange messages independently of each other, enabling real-time data exchange.

Key Features of Websockets

1. **Full-Duplex Communication**: Both the client and server can send and receive messages simultaneously.
2. **Persistent Connection**: The connection remains open, eliminating the need for repeated handshakes.
3. **Low Latency**: Ideal for applications requiring immediate feedback.
4. **Lightweight**: Messages are transmitted with minimal overhead compared to HTTP.

How Do Websockets Work?

1. **Handshake**
   The Websocket connection begins with an HTTP handshake. If successful, the protocol upgrades to Websocket.
2. **Persistent Connection**
   Once established, the connection remains open, allowing bidirectional communication.
3. **Message Exchange**
   Messages can be exchanged in real time between the client and server without the need for repeated requests.

Use Cases for Websockets

Websockets are particularly useful for:

- **Chat Applications**: Enabling users to send and receive messages in real time.
- **Live Notifications**: Providing instant updates for events, such as emails or alerts.
- **Collaborative Tools**: Supporting real-time collaboration in tools like Google Docs.
- **Online Gaming**: Facilitating low-latency communication between players.
- **Live Streaming**: Streaming data such as stock prices, sports scores, or video feeds.

Websockets vs. HTTP

Feature	HTTP	Websockets
Communication Type	Request-Response	Full-Duplex
Connection	Short-Lived	Persistent

Latency	High (due to repeated handshakes)	Low
Overhead	Higher	Lower

Setting Up a Basic Websocket in Go

Let's start with a simple example to establish a Websocket connection in Go.

Step 1: Install the Gorilla Websocket Package

The `gorilla/websocket` package is a popular library for handling Websockets in Go.

bash

```
go get github.com/gorilla/websocket
```

Step 2: Write the Websocket Server

File: `main.go`

go

```
package main
```

```go
import (

    "fmt"

    "net/http"

    "github.com/gorilla/websocket"

)


var upgrader = websocket.Upgrader{

    CheckOrigin: func(r *http.Request) bool {

        return true // Allow all origins for
simplicity

    },

}

func handleWebsocket(w http.ResponseWriter, r
*http.Request) {

    conn, err := upgrader.Upgrade(w, r, nil)

    if err != nil {

        fmt.Println("Error          upgrading
connection:", err)

        return
```

```go
    }

    defer conn.Close()


    for {

        messageType,    message,    err    :=
conn.ReadMessage()

        if err != nil {

            fmt.Println("Error         reading
message:", err)

            break

        }


        fmt.Printf("Received:          %s\n",
message)


        if                err                :=
conn.WriteMessage(messageType, message); err
!= nil {

            fmt.Println("Error         writing
message:", err)
```

```go
            break
        }
    }
}


func main() {

    http.HandleFunc("/ws", handleWebsocket)


    fmt.Println("Server started on :8080")

    err := http.ListenAndServe(":8080", nil)

    if err != nil {

        fmt.Println("Error              starting
server:", err)

    }

}
```

Step 3: Create a Simple Client

File: `index.html`

html

```
<!DOCTYPE html>

<html lang="en">

<head>

    <meta charset="UTF-8">

    <meta                        name="viewport"
content="width=device-width,       initial-
scale=1.0">

    <title>Websocket Example</title>

</head>

<body>

    <h1>Websocket Demo</h1>

    <input      id="message"      type="text"
placeholder="Enter a message">

    <button
onclick="sendMessage()">Send</button>

    <div id="output"></div>
```

```
<script>

    const        ws         =         new
WebSocket("ws://localhost:8080/ws");

    ws.onmessage = function(event) {

        const          output          =
document.getElementById("output");

        const         message          =
document.createElement("div");

        message.textContent = "Server: "
+ event.data;

        output.appendChild(message);

    };


    function sendMessage() {

        const          input           =
document.getElementById("message");

        ws.send(input.value);

        input.value = "";

    }
```

```
    </script>

  </body>

  </html>
```

Step 4: Run the Application

Start the Go server:
bash

```
go run main.go
```

1. Open `index.html` in a browser.
2. Enter a message and observe real-time communication.

Practical Exercise

Task: Modify the above example to broadcast messages to all connected clients.

Hints:

- Use a `map` to store active connections.
- Implement a `for` loop to send messages to all clients.

8.2 Building a Real-Time Chat Application in Go

Real-time chat applications are one of the most common use cases for Websockets. In this chapter, we will build a real-time chat application in Go. This application will allow multiple users to join a chat room, send messages, and see messages from others in real-time.

Understanding the Architecture

Before diving into the code, let's outline the architecture of our chat application:

1. **Websocket Server**: Handles incoming Websocket connections and manages the communication between clients.
2. **Message Broadcasting**: Ensures that messages from one client are sent to all connected clients.
3. **Client Interface**: A simple web page where users can send and receive messages.

Step 1: Setting Up the Websocket Server

We will use the `gorilla/websocket` package to manage Websocket connections.

Install the Package

bash

```
go get github.com/gorilla/websocket
```

Code the Server

File: `main.go`

go

```go
package main

import (

    "fmt"

    "net/http"

    "sync"


    "github.com/gorilla/websocket"
)
// Upgrader to handle Websocket connections

var upgrader = websocket.Upgrader{

    CheckOrigin: func(r *http.Request) bool {

        return true // Allow all origins for
simplicity
```

```go
        },
    }

// Client struct to represent each connected
client

type Client struct {

    conn *websocket.Conn

    send chan []byte

}

// ChatHub struct to manage clients and
broadcasting

type ChatHub struct {

    clients     map[*Client]bool

    broadcast   chan []byte

    register    chan *Client

    unregister  chan *Client

    mu          sync.Mutex

}

// NewChatHub creates a new ChatHub instance
```

```go
func NewChatHub() *ChatHub {

    return &ChatHub{

        clients:    make(map[*Client]bool),

        broadcast:  make(chan []byte),

        register:   make(chan *Client),

        unregister: make(chan *Client),

    }

}

// Run starts the ChatHub to handle events

func (hub *ChatHub) Run() {

    for {

        select {

        case client := <-hub.register:

            hub.mu.Lock()

            hub.clients[client] = true

            hub.mu.Unlock()


        case client := <-hub.unregister:
```

```go
            hub.mu.Lock()

            if _, ok := hub.clients[client];
ok {

                delete(hub.clients, client)

                close(client.send)

            }

            hub.mu.Unlock()


        case message := <-hub.broadcast:

            hub.mu.Lock()

            for client := range hub.clients {

                select {

                case client.send <- message:

                default:

                    close(client.send)

                    delete(hub.clients,
client)

                }
```

```go
        }

        hub.mu.Unlock()

    }

}


// HandleConnections handles incoming
Websocket connections

func (hub *ChatHub) HandleConnections(w
http.ResponseWriter, r *http.Request) {

    conn, err := upgrader.Upgrade(w, r, nil)

    if err != nil {

        fmt.Println("Error          upgrading
connection:", err)

        return

    }

    client := &Client{conn: conn, send:
make(chan []byte)}

    hub.register <- client
```

```go
    go hub.handleMessages(client)


    defer func() {

        hub.unregister <- client

        conn.Close()

    }()


    for message := range client.send {

        if              err              :=
conn.WriteMessage(websocket.TextMessage,
message); err != nil {

            break

        }

    }

}


// handleMessages reads messages from a
client and broadcasts them
```

```go
func (hub *ChatHub) handleMessages(client
*Client) {
    defer func() {
        hub.unregister <- client
        client.conn.Close()
    }()
    for {
        _, message, err :=
client.conn.ReadMessage()
        if err != nil {
            break
        }
        hub.broadcast <- message
    }
}
func main() {
    hub := NewChatHub()
    go hub.Run()
```

```go
    http.HandleFunc("/ws",
hub.HandleConnections)

    fmt.Println("Server started on :8080")

    err := http.ListenAndServe(":8080", nil)

    if err != nil {

        fmt.Println("Error                starting
server:", err)

    }

}
```

Step 2: Creating the Client Interface

The client interface will allow users to send messages and see messages from others in real time.

File: `index.html`

html

```html
<!DOCTYPE html>

<html lang="en">

<head>

    <meta charset="UTF-8">
```

```
<meta                         name="viewport"
content="width=device-width,         initial-
scale=1.0">

<title>Chat Room</title>

<style>

    body {

        font-family: Arial, sans-serif;

        margin: 20px;

    }

    #chat {

        border: 1px solid #ccc;

        padding: 10px;

        height: 300px;

        overflow-y: scroll;

    }

    #message {

        width: 80%;

        padding: 10px;
```

```
        }

        #send {

            padding: 10px;

        }

    </style>

</head>

<body>

    <h1>Real-Time Chat Room</h1>

    <div id="chat"></div>

    <input      id="message"      type="text"
placeholder="Type your message">

    <button id="send">Send</button>

    <script>

        const      ws      =      new
WebSocket("ws://localhost:8080/ws");


        const           chat           =
document.getElementById("chat");
```

```javascript
      const          messageInput      =
document.getElementById("message");

      const          sendButton        =
document.getElementById("send");


      ws.onmessage = function(event) {

        const          message          =
document.createElement("div");

        message.textContent            =
event.data;

        chat.appendChild(message);

        chat.scrollTop                 =
chat.scrollHeight;

      };


      sendButton.addEventListener("click",
function() {

        const          message          =
messageInput.value;

        ws.send(message);
```

```javascript
        messageInput.value = "";

    });



messageInput.addEventListener("keypress",
function(event) {

        if (event.key === "Enter") {

            sendButton.click();

        }

    });

</script>

</body>

</html>
```

Step 3: Running the Application

Start the Go server:

bash

417

```
go run main.go
```

1. **Open the client interface**: Open `index.html` in a web browser.
2. **Test the chat**: Open the page in multiple browser tabs or devices and test the real-time messaging.

8.3 Managing Concurrent Connections with Goroutines

Concurrency is one of Go's most powerful features. It enables developers to handle multiple tasks simultaneously, which is particularly useful in real-time applications like chat systems, gaming platforms, or collaborative tools. In this chapter, we'll explore how to manage concurrent Websocket connections using Goroutines effectively.

Understanding Concurrency in Go

Concurrency in Go is achieved using Goroutines and channels.

- **Goroutines**: Lightweight threads managed by Go's runtime. They are created using the `go` keyword.
- **Channels**: Allow communication between Goroutines to synchronize data and actions.

Why Concurrency Matters for Websockets

In a Websocket server, multiple clients can connect simultaneously. Each client needs to send and receive messages independently of others. Managing these connections concurrently ensures the server remains responsive and scalable.

Step 1: Setting Up a Websocket Server with Concurrent Connections

Let's build a simple Websocket server that can handle multiple clients concurrently.

Code Example: Websocket Server

File: `main.go`

```go
package main

import (

    "fmt"

    "net/http"

    "sync"
```

```go
    "github.com/gorilla/websocket"
)
// Upgrader to handle Websocket connections
var upgrader = websocket.Upgrader{
    CheckOrigin: func(r *http.Request) bool {
        return true // Allow all origins for
simplicity
    },
}
// Client struct to represent each connected
client
type Client struct {
    conn *websocket.Conn
    send chan []byte
}
// ChatHub struct to manage clients and
broadcasting
type ChatHub struct {
    clients    map[*Client]bool
```

```go
    broadcast   chan []byte

    register    chan *Client

    unregister  chan *Client

    mu          sync.Mutex

}

// NewChatHub creates a new ChatHub instance

func NewChatHub() *ChatHub {

    return &ChatHub{

        clients:    make(map[*Client]bool),

        broadcast:  make(chan []byte),

        register:   make(chan *Client),

        unregister: make(chan *Client),

    }

}

// Run starts the ChatHub to handle events
concurrently

func (hub *ChatHub) Run() {

    for {
```

```go
select {
case client := <-hub.register:
    hub.mu.Lock()
    hub.clients[client] = true
    hub.mu.Unlock()
    fmt.Println("New              client
registered")
    case client := <-hub.unregister:
        hub.mu.Lock()
        if _, ok := hub.clients[client];
ok {
            delete(hub.clients, client)
            close(client.send)
            fmt.Println("Client
unregistered")
        }
        hub.mu.Unlock()
    case message := <-hub.broadcast:
        hub.mu.Lock()
```

```go
        for client := range hub.clients {

            select {

            case client.send <- message:

            default:

                close(client.send)

                delete(hub.clients,
client)

            }

        }

        hub.mu.Unlock()

    }

}

// HandleConnections handles incoming
Websocket connections

func (hub *ChatHub) HandleConnections(w
http.ResponseWriter, r *http.Request) {

    conn, err := upgrader.Upgrade(w, r, nil)

    if err != nil {
```

```go
        fmt.Println("Error          upgrading
connection:", err)

        return

    }

    client  :=  &Client{conn:  conn,  send:
make(chan []byte)}

    hub.register <- client

    go hub.handleMessages(client)

    defer func() {

        hub.unregister <- client

        conn.Close()

    }()


    for message := range client.send {

        if            err                :=
conn.WriteMessage(websocket.TextMessage,
message); err != nil {

            break

        }
```

```go
    }

}

// handleMessages reads messages from a
client and broadcasts them

func (hub *ChatHub) handleMessages(client
*Client) {

    defer func() {

        hub.unregister <- client

        client.conn.Close()

    }()


    for {

        _,       message,       err       :=
client.conn.ReadMessage()

        if err != nil {

            break

        }

        hub.broadcast <- message

    }
```

```go
}


func main() {

    hub := NewChatHub()

    go hub.Run()


    http.HandleFunc("/ws",
hub.HandleConnections)


    fmt.Println("Server started on :8080")

    err := http.ListenAndServe(":8080", nil)

    if err != nil {

        fmt.Println("Error          starting
server:", err)

    }

}
```

Step 2: Managing Goroutines Safely

Avoiding Race Conditions

When multiple Goroutines access shared resources (like the `clients` map), race conditions can occur. To prevent this:

- Use `sync.Mutex` to lock and unlock resources during updates.

Use Go's `race detector` to identify potential issues during development:
bash

```
go run -race main.go
```

Step 3: Scaling the Server

Optimizing Goroutines

- **Connection Limits**: Set a maximum number of clients to prevent overloading the server.
- **Timeouts**: Implement timeouts for inactive connections to free up resources.

Code Example: Connection Timeout

go

```go
conn.SetReadDeadline(time.Now().Add(60      *
time.Second))

conn.SetPongHandler(func(string) error {

    conn.SetReadDeadline(time.Now().Add(60  *
time.Second))

    return nil

})
```

Step 4: Testing Concurrent Connections

Simulating Multiple Clients

You can use tools like Websocket Client or write a script to simulate multiple connections.

File: `client_simulation.go`

go

```go
package main

import (

    "fmt"

    "log"

    "net/url"
```

```go
    "github.com/gorilla/websocket"
)

func main() {

    serverURL := url.URL{Scheme: "ws", Host:
"localhost:8080", Path: "/ws"}

    conn,          _,          err          :=
websocket.DefaultDialer.Dial(serverURL.Strin
g(), nil)

    if err != nil {

        log.Fatal("Error connecting:", err)

    }

    defer conn.Close()


    for i := 0; i < 10; i++ {

        message := fmt.Sprintf("Message %d",
i+1)

        err                                 :=
conn.WriteMessage(websocket.TextMessage,
[]byte(message))
```

```
if err != nil {

    log.Println("Write error:", err)

    return

}

}

}
```

Hands-On Project: Develop a simple chat room application where multiple users can send and receive messages in real-time.

In this hands-on project, we will develop a real-time chat room application where multiple users can connect, send, and receive messages simultaneously. This project leverages Websockets for real-time communication and Go's concurrency features to handle multiple connections efficiently.

Project Goals

1. Build a Websocket server to handle multiple clients.
2. Allow users to send and receive messages in real-time.
3. Use Goroutines to manage concurrent connections.
4. Implement a chat hub to broadcast messages to all connected clients.

Prerequisites

Before starting, ensure you have the following:

1. **Go installed**: Download and install Go.

Gorilla Websocket package: Install it using the command: bash

```
go get -u github.com/gorilla/websocket
```

Step 1: Project Setup

Create a new directory for your project:
bash

```
mkdir go-chat-app
cd go-chat-app
```

Initialize a Go module:
bash

```
go mod init go-chat-app
```

Step 2: Define the Chat Hub

The chat hub manages all connected clients and handles broadcasting messages.

File: `hub.go`

go

```go
package main

import (

    "sync"

)

// Client represents a connected user

type Client struct {

    conn *websocket.Conn

    send chan []byte

}

// ChatHub manages all clients and broadcasts
messages

type ChatHub struct {

    clients    map[*Client]bool
```

```go
    broadcast   chan []byte

    register    chan *Client

    unregister chan *Client

    mu          sync.Mutex
}
// NewChatHub creates a new ChatHub instance
func NewChatHub() *ChatHub {

    return &ChatHub{

        clients:    make(map[*Client]bool),

        broadcast:  make(chan []byte),

        register:   make(chan *Client),

        unregister: make(chan *Client),

    }

}
// Run starts the hub to handle client events
func (hub *ChatHub) Run() {

    for {

        select {
```
433

```go
        case client := <-hub.register:

            hub.mu.Lock()

            hub.clients[client] = true

            hub.mu.Unlock()


        case client := <-hub.unregister:

            hub.mu.Lock()

            if _, ok := hub.clients[client];
ok {

                delete(hub.clients, client)

                close(client.send)

            }

            hub.mu.Unlock()


        case message := <-hub.broadcast:

            hub.mu.Lock()

            for client := range hub.clients {

                select {
```

```go
                case client.send <- message:

                default:

                    close(client.send)

                    delete(hub.clients,
client)

                }

            }

            hub.mu.Unlock()

        }

    }

}
```

Step 3: Websocket Server

The server handles Websocket connections and communicates with the chat hub.

File: `server.go`

go

```go
package main

import (

    "fmt"

    "net/http"

    "github.com/gorilla/websocket"

)

// Upgrader upgrades HTTP connections to
Websockets

var upgrader = websocket.Upgrader{

    CheckOrigin: func(r *http.Request) bool {

        return true // Allow all origins for
simplicity

    },

}

// HandleConnections handles incoming
Websocket connections

func (hub *ChatHub) HandleConnections(w
http.ResponseWriter, r *http.Request) {
```

```go
    conn, err := upgrader.Upgrade(w, r, nil)

    if err != nil {

        fmt.Println("Error          upgrading
connection:", err)

        return

    }

    client   :=   &Client{conn:   conn,   send:
make(chan []byte)}

    hub.register <- client

    go hub.handleMessages(client)


    defer func() {

        hub.unregister <- client

        conn.Close()

    }()


    for message := range client.send {
```

```go
        if            err           :=
conn.WriteMessage(websocket.TextMessage,
message); err != nil {

            break

        }

    }

}

// handleMessages reads messages from a
client and broadcasts them

func (hub *ChatHub) handleMessages(client
*Client) {

    defer func() {

        hub.unregister <- client

        client.conn.Close()

    }()


    for {

        _,       message,       err       :=
client.conn.ReadMessage()
```

```go
        if err != nil {

            break

        }

        hub.broadcast <- message

    }

}
```

Step 4: Main Application

File: `main.go`

go

```go
package main

import (

    "fmt"

    "net/http"
```

```go
)

func main() {

    hub := NewChatHub()

    go hub.Run()

    http.HandleFunc("/ws",
hub.HandleConnections)

    fmt.Println("Server started on :8080")

    err := http.ListenAndServe(":8080", nil)

    if err != nil {

        fmt.Println("Error          starting
server:", err)

    }

}
```

Step 5: Testing the Application

Run the server:
bash
```
go run main.go hub.go server.go
```

1. Open a Websocket client tool like <u>WebSocket King</u> or create a simple HTML client:

File: `client.html`

html

```
<!DOCTYPE html>

<html>

<head>

    <title>Chat Room</title>

</head>

<body>

    <h1>Chat Room</h1>

    <textarea    id="messages"    rows="20"
cols="50" readonly></textarea><br>

    <input    type="text"    id="message"
placeholder="Type your message" />

    <button
onclick="sendMessage()">Send</button>

    <script>
```

```javascript
        const       socket       =       new
WebSocket("ws://localhost:8080/ws");

        socket.onmessage = function(event) {

            const          messages          =
document.getElementById("messages");

            messages.value  +=  event.data  +
"\n";

        };


        function sendMessage() {

            const           input           =
document.getElementById("message");

            socket.send(input.value);

            input.value = "";

        }
```
    </script>

</body>

</html>

3. Open `client.html` in multiple browser tabs and start chatting!

Key Concepts Explained

1. **Websocket Connections**: Persistent connections allowing two-way communication between client and server.
2. **Goroutines**: Used for handling concurrent client connections.
3. **Channels**: Enable communication between Goroutines for broadcasting messages.
4. **Synchronization**: `sync.Mutex` ensures safe access to shared resources.

Enhancements to Try

1. Add **usernames** to identify users in the chat.
2. Implement **message history** using a database.
3. Add **private messaging** between users.

Chapter 9: Deployment and Scaling

Building a web application is only part of the journey; deploying it to a production environment and ensuring it can handle traffic efficiently are equally critical. In this chapter, we'll explore the deployment of Go applications to cloud platforms, containerization with Docker, scaling using load balancers, and monitoring for optimal performance.

9.1 Deploying Go Applications to Cloud Platforms (AWS, GCP, Heroku)

Deploying your Go application to a cloud platform is a critical step in making it accessible to users worldwide. In this chapter, we'll explore how to deploy a Go application to three popular cloud platforms: AWS, Google Cloud Platform (GCP), and Heroku. By the end, you'll have a clear understanding of deployment workflows, best practices, and how to choose the right platform for your needs.

Why Deploy to the Cloud?

Cloud platforms provide scalable, reliable, and cost-effective infrastructure to host your applications. Benefits include:

- **Scalability**: Handle increased traffic seamlessly.
- **Global Reach**: Serve users from data centers worldwide.
- **Managed Services**: Reduce operational overhead.

444

Preparing Your Go Application for Deployment

Before deploying, ensure your Go application is production-ready:

Build a Binary: Compile your Go application to a binary using: bash

```
go build -o app
```

1. **Environment Variables**: Use environment variables for configuration (e.g., database credentials).

Port Configuration: Ensure your app listens on a configurable port: go

```
port := os.Getenv("PORT")

if port == "" {

    port = "8080"

}

log.Fatal(http.ListenAndServe(":"+port,
nil))
```

Deploying to Heroku

Heroku is a beginner-friendly platform ideal for quick deployments.

Step 1: Install Heroku CLI

Download and install the Heroku CLI from Heroku CLI.

Step 2: Login to Heroku

Authenticate with Heroku:

bash

```
heroku login
```

Step 3: Create a `Procfile`

Heroku uses a `Procfile` to define how your app runs: **File: `Procfile`**

plaintext

```
web: ./app
```

Step 4: Initialize a Git Repository

Ensure your project is version-controlled:

bash

```
git init
git add .
```

```
git commit -m "Initial commit"
```

Step 5: Create a Heroku App

Create a new Heroku app:

bash

```
heroku create
```

Step 6: Deploy Your Application

Push your code to Heroku:

bash

```
git push heroku main
```

Step 7: Access Your Application

Heroku provides a URL for your app:

bash

```
heroku open
```

Deploying to AWS (Elastic Beanstalk)

AWS provides flexible infrastructure for scalable applications.

Step 1: Install AWS CLI

Download and install the AWS CLI from AWS CLI.

Step 2: Configure AWS CLI

Set up your AWS credentials:

bash

```
aws configure
```

Step 3: Install Elastic Beanstalk CLI

Install the Elastic Beanstalk CLI:

bash

```
pip install awsebcli
```

Step 4: Initialize Elastic Beanstalk

Run the following command in your project directory:

bash

```
eb init
```

- Choose your region.
- Select a platform (Go).

Step 5: Create an Environment

Create an Elastic Beanstalk environment:

bash

```
eb create my-app-env
```

Step 6: Deploy Your Application

Deploy your app:

bash

```
eb deploy
```

Step 7: Access Your Application

Get the environment URL:

bash

```
eb open
```

Deploying to Google Cloud Platform (GCP)

GCP offers a range of services, including App Engine for easy deployment.

Step 1: Install gcloud CLI

Download and install the Google Cloud CLI from gcloud CLI.

Step 2: Authenticate and Configure

Authenticate and set your project:

bash

```
gcloud auth login

gcloud config set project [PROJECT_ID]
```

Step 3: Create an `app.yaml`

Define your app configuration: **File:** `app.yaml`

yaml

```
runtime: go120

instance_class: F1
```

Step 4: Deploy Your Application

Deploy using:

bash

```
gcloud app deploy
```

Step 5: Access Your Application

View your app:

bash

```
gcloud app browse
```

Practical Exercise

Let's deploy a simple Go web server to Heroku, AWS, and GCP.

Step 1: Create a Simple Web Server

File: `main.go`

go

```
package main
```

```go
import (

    "fmt"

    "log"

    "net/http"

    "os"

)

func handler(w http.ResponseWriter, r
*http.Request) {

    fmt.Fprintln(w, "Hello, World!")

}

func main() {

    port := os.Getenv("PORT")

    if port == "" {

        port = "8080"

    }

    http.HandleFunc("/", handler)

    log.Printf("Server starting on port
%s\n", port)
```

```
    log.Fatal(http.ListenAndServe(":"+port,
nil))

}
```

Step 2: Test Locally

Run your application:

bash

```
go run main.go
```

Visit `http://localhost:8080`.

Step 3: Deploy

Follow the steps above for Heroku, AWS, or GCP.

Best Practices for Cloud Deployment

1. **Environment Variables**: Never hardcode sensitive data.
2. **Logging**: Use structured logging for easier debugging.
3. **Scaling**: Use cloud auto-scaling to handle traffic spikes.
4. **Security**: Secure credentials using tools like AWS Secrets Manager or GCP Secret Manager.

9.2 Containerization with Docker

Containerization has become a key concept in modern software development. Docker, one of the most popular containerization tools, allows you to package your application and its dependencies into a standardized unit called a container. This makes it easier to develop, ship, and run applications consistently across different environments. In this chapter, we'll explore how to containerize a Go application using Docker and explain the fundamental concepts behind Docker containers.

What is Docker?

Docker is an open-source platform that automates the deployment, scaling, and management of applications inside lightweight containers. Containers are isolated environments that run your application along with all its dependencies, ensuring that it works the same way across different machines.

Why Use Docker?

- **Consistency**: Docker containers provide a consistent environment, eliminating the "it works on my machine" problem.

- **Portability**: Once you package your application in a container, you can run it anywhere—on your local machine, on a cloud server, or in a production environment.
- **Scalability**: Docker containers are lightweight and can be easily replicated, making it easier to scale your application.

Understanding Docker Basics

Before we dive into containerizing a Go application, let's quickly cover some key Docker concepts:

- **Image**: A read-only template used to create containers. It contains the application and its dependencies.
- **Container**: A running instance of an image. It is an isolated environment that runs the application.
- **Dockerfile**: A text file that contains instructions on how to build a Docker image for your application.

Setting Up Docker for Go Applications

Step 1: Install Docker

To begin, you need to install Docker on your system. Visit Docker's official website and follow the installation instructions for your operating system.

After installation, verify that Docker is installed correctly by running:

bash

```
docker --version
```

Step 2: Create a Simple Go Application

Let's create a simple Go application that we will later containerize.

File: `main.go`

go

```go
package main

import (

    "fmt"

    "net/http"

    "os"

)

func    handler(w     http.ResponseWriter,     r
*http.Request) {

    fmt.Fprintf(w, "Hello from Go inside a
Docker container!")

}
```

```go
func main() {

    port := os.Getenv("PORT")

    if port == "" {

        port = "8080"

    }

    http.HandleFunc("/", handler)

    fmt.Printf("Server is running on port %s\n", port)

    http.ListenAndServe(":"+port, nil)

}
```

This Go application listens on a configurable port and responds with a simple message when accessed.

Step 3: Writing the Dockerfile

The Dockerfile defines the steps to create a Docker image for your application. Here's how we can containerize the Go application:

File: `Dockerfile`

Dockerfile

```dockerfile
# Step 1: Use the official Go image as a base
FROM golang:1.19-alpine

# Step 2: Set the working directory inside
the container
WORKDIR /app

# Step 3: Copy the Go module files and
download dependencies
COPY go.mod go.sum ./
RUN go mod download

# Step 4: Copy the Go source code into the
container
COPY . .

# Step 5: Build the Go application
RUN go build -o app .
```

```
# Step 6: Expose the port the app will run on

EXPOSE 8080


# Step 7: Define the command to run the
application

CMD ["./app"]
```

Explanation of Each Step:

1. **FROM golang:1.19-alpine**: This specifies the base image. We use an official Go image based on Alpine Linux, which is lightweight.
2. **WORKDIR /app**: This sets the working directory inside the container to `/app`.
3. **COPY go.mod go.sum ./**: This copies the Go module files into the container. This step ensures that Go dependencies are installed in the next step.
4. **RUN go mod download**: This downloads the Go dependencies.
5. **COPY . .**: This copies the source code from the host machine into the container.
6. **RUN go build -o app .**: This builds the Go application inside the container.

7. **EXPOSE 8080**: This tells Docker that the container will listen on port 8080.
8. **CMD ["./app"]**: This specifies the command to run when the container starts. It runs the Go application.

Step 4: Building the Docker Image

Now that we have the Dockerfile, we can build the Docker image for our Go application. In the directory containing your `Dockerfile` and `main.go`, run the following command:

bash

```
docker build -t go-chat-app .
```

This command will:

- Read the `Dockerfile` in the current directory (`.`).
- Build an image named `go-chat-app`.

After the build completes, you can check the image with:

bash

```
docker images
```

Step 5: Running the Docker Container

Once the image is built, you can run the container with the following command:

bash

```
docker run -p 8080:8080 go-chat-app
```

This will:

- Start a container from the `go-chat-app` image.
- Map port 8080 on your local machine to port 8080 inside the container.

Now, visit `http://localhost:8080` in your browser. You should see the message "Hello from Go inside a Docker container!"

Step 6: Docker Compose (Optional)

If your application depends on other services (e.g., a database), you can use Docker Compose to define and run multi-container Docker applications.

File: `docker-compose.yml`

yaml

```
version: '3'

services:
```

```
app:

  build: .

  ports:

    - "8080:8080"
```

This `docker-compose.yml` file will build the Go app image and run it on port 8080.

To start the app with Docker Compose:

bash

```
docker-compose up
```

Step 7: Pushing the Docker Image to a Registry

Once your application is containerized, you may want to push the image to a container registry (e.g., Docker Hub) for easy deployment.

Login to Docker Hub:
bash
```
docker login
```

Tag the Image: Tag your image with your Docker Hub username:

bash

```
docker tag go-chat-app yourusername/go-chat-app
```

Push the Image: Push the image to Docker Hub:
bash

```
docker push yourusername/go-chat-app
```

Now, your image is available on Docker Hub, and you can pull it from any machine:

bash

```
docker pull yourusername/go-chat-app
```

Best Practices for Dockerizing Go Applications

- **Minimize Image Size**: Use smaller base images like `alpine` to reduce the size of your Docker images.
- **Multi-stage Builds**: Use multi-stage builds to separate the build environment from the runtime environment. This reduces the size of the final image.
- **Health Checks**: Implement health checks in your Dockerfile to ensure your application is running correctly.
- **Environment Variables**: Use environment variables for configuration, especially for sensitive data like API keys or database credentials.

9.3 Scaling Web Applications with Load Balancers

As your web application grows, you may encounter the need to handle an increasing number of requests from users. This is where scaling comes into play. One of the most effective ways to scale web applications is by using **load balancers**. In this chapter, we will explore what load balancing is, why it's important, and how to implement it for Go applications. We will also cover various types of load balancing strategies and provide a practical example of scaling a Go web application with a load balancer.

What is Load Balancing?

Load balancing is the process of distributing incoming network traffic across multiple servers. The goal is to ensure that no single server is overwhelmed with too many requests, which can lead to slower response times or even downtime. By balancing the load, you can improve the availability, reliability, and performance of your web application.

A **load balancer** is a device or software that sits between clients and your servers, routing incoming requests to the appropriate server based on various criteria.

Why Use Load Balancers?

- **Scalability**: Load balancers enable you to scale your application horizontally by adding more servers (instances) to handle increased traffic.
- **High Availability**: If one server fails, the load balancer can redirect traffic to healthy servers, ensuring continuous availability of your application.
- **Improved Performance**: By distributing requests efficiently, load balancers help reduce the load on individual servers, leading to faster response times.

Types of Load Balancing

There are several types of load balancing algorithms that determine how the load balancer distributes traffic to backend servers:

1. **Round Robin**: The load balancer distributes requests evenly across all servers in a sequential manner.
2. **Least Connections**: The load balancer directs traffic to the server with the fewest active connections.
3. **IP Hash**: The load balancer uses the client's IP address to determine which server should handle the request.
4. **Weighted Load Balancing**: Servers are assigned weights based on their capacity, and traffic is distributed accordingly.

Setting Up Load Balancing for a Go Web Application

Let's go through the steps of scaling a simple Go web application using a load balancer. We will use **Nginx** as our load balancer, a popular and efficient tool for distributing traffic.

Step 1: Create a Simple Go Web Application

We will use the same Go web application from the previous chapter. This simple app listens on port 8080 and responds with a message indicating which server handled the request.

File: `main.go`

```go
package main

import (

    "fmt"

    "net/http"

    "os"

)

func handler(w http.ResponseWriter, r *http.Request) {

    serverName := os.Getenv("SERVER_NAME")
```

```go
    fmt.Fprintf(w,      "Hello      from      Go
application running on %s", serverName)
}

func main() {

    port := os.Getenv("PORT")

    if port == "" {

        port = "8080"

    }

    http.HandleFunc("/", handler)

    http.ListenAndServe(":"+port, nil)

}
```

This application will return the server's name as part of the response to identify which instance is handling the request.

Step 2: Dockerizing the Application

We'll containerize the Go application, so we can easily replicate it across multiple instances.

File: `Dockerfile`

Dockerfile

```
FROM golang:1.19-alpine

WORKDIR /app

COPY go.mod go.sum ./

RUN go mod download


COPY . .

RUN go build -o app .


EXPOSE 8080

CMD ["./app"]
```

Build the Docker image:

bash

```
docker build -t go-load-balancing .
```

Step 3: Running Multiple Instances of the Go Application

Now that we have the Docker image, we can run multiple instances of the Go application. Each instance will be running in its own container, and we will assign a unique SERVER_NAME environment variable to each instance to distinguish them.

Run the first instance:

bash

```
docker run -d -e SERVER_NAME="Server 1" -p 8081:8080 go-load-balancing
```

Run the second instance:

bash

```
docker run -d -e SERVER_NAME="Server 2" -p 8082:8080 go-load-balancing
```

Now we have two instances of the Go application running on ports 8081 and 8082.

Step 4: Setting Up Nginx as a Load Balancer

Next, we'll set up Nginx to distribute incoming requests between the two Go application instances. Nginx will act as the load balancer.

File: `nginx.conf`

nginx

```
http {

    upstream go_app {

        server 127.0.0.1:8081;

        server 127.0.0.1:8082;

    }

    server {

        listen 80;


        location / {

            proxy_pass http://go_app;

            proxy_set_header Host $host;

            proxy_set_header      X-Real-IP
$remote_addr;

            proxy_set_header X-Forwarded-For
$proxy_add_x_forwarded_for;

        }
```

```
        }
}
```

This configuration tells Nginx to balance the load between two servers running on ports 8081 and 8082.

Step 5: Running Nginx

Now, we'll run Nginx using Docker and bind it to port 80 on the host machine.

Create a `Dockerfile` for Nginx:

File: `Dockerfile.nginx`

Dockerfile

```
FROM nginx:alpine

COPY nginx.conf /etc/nginx/nginx.conf
```

Build the Nginx image:

bash

```
docker   build   -t   go-load-balancer   -f
Dockerfile.nginx .
```

Run the Nginx container:

bash

```
docker run -d -p 80:80 --link go-load-
balancing go-load-balancer
```

Step 6: Testing the Load Balancer

Now that everything is set up, we can test the load balancer. Visit `http://localhost` in your browser. You should see alternating responses from `Server 1` and `Server 2`, indicating that Nginx is distributing traffic between the two Go application instances.

You can also use a tool like `curl` to test this:

bash

```
curl http://localhost
```

Repeat the command several times to see the load balancing in action.

Step 7: Scaling the Application

If you need to scale the application further, you can run more instances of the Go application and update the Nginx configuration to include the new instances.

For example, to add a third instance:

472

bash

```bash
docker run -d -e SERVER_NAME="Server 3" -p 8083:8080 go-load-balancing
```

Then, update the `nginx.conf` file to include the new instance:

nginx

```nginx
upstream go_app {
    server 127.0.0.1:8081;
    server 127.0.0.1:8082;
    server 127.0.0.1:8083;
}
```

After making this change, reload Nginx:

bash

```bash
docker exec -it <nginx_container_id> nginx -s reload
```

Now, the load balancer will distribute traffic across three Go application instances.

Best Practices for Load Balancing

- **Health Checks**: Implement health checks to ensure that the load balancer only sends traffic to healthy servers. Nginx can be configured to check the health of backend servers.

- **Sticky Sessions**: If your application requires session persistence, configure sticky sessions to route requests from the same client to the same server.

- **SSL Termination**: Use Nginx to terminate SSL connections, ensuring secure communication between clients and your load balancer.

- **Auto-Scaling**: In cloud environments, use auto-scaling groups to automatically add or remove instances based on traffic demand.

9.4 Monitoring and Logging for Web Applications

In the world of modern web development, it's essential to keep track of your application's performance, errors, and user behavior. Monitoring and logging provide insights that help ensure your application is running smoothly, detect issues early, and improve the overall user experience. In this chapter, we will explore how to set up monitoring and logging for your Go web applications, helping you maintain high availability and performance.

What is Monitoring and Logging?

- **Monitoring**: Monitoring refers to the practice of continuously tracking the health and performance of your application. This includes tracking metrics like response times, error rates, and resource usage (CPU, memory, etc.). Monitoring helps you detect issues before they affect your users.

- **Logging**: Logging is the process of recording events that occur within your application. These events can be errors, system events, or user interactions. Logs are essential for debugging, troubleshooting, and understanding how users interact with your application.

Together, monitoring and logging form the foundation of a reliable and maintainable application.

Why Monitoring and Logging Are Important

- **Proactive Issue Detection**: Monitoring helps you detect problems before they escalate, while logs provide detailed information to diagnose and resolve issues.

- **Performance Optimization**: By tracking performance metrics, you can identify bottlenecks in your application and optimize them for better user experience.

- **Audit Trails**: Logs provide a historical record of events, which is useful for debugging, troubleshooting, and even security audits.

Setting Up Monitoring for Go Applications

To effectively monitor your Go web application, you need to track various metrics like HTTP request rates, response times, and error rates. There are many monitoring tools available, but for simplicity, we will integrate **Prometheus** and **Grafana**, two widely used open-source tools for monitoring and visualization.

Step 1: Install Prometheus and Grafana

1. **Prometheus** is an open-source monitoring system that collects and stores metrics in a time-series database.
2. **Grafana** is a powerful visualization tool that integrates with Prometheus to display the collected metrics.

To install Prometheus and Grafana, follow the instructions on their official websites:

- Prometheus Installation Guide
- Grafana Installation Guide

Step 2: Integrating Prometheus with Your Go Application

To expose metrics from your Go application, you need to integrate the **Prometheus Go client**. This client allows your application to expose HTTP endpoints that Prometheus can scrape to collect metrics.

Install the Prometheus Go client:
bash

```
go get
github.com/prometheus/client_golang/prometheus

go                                          get
github.com/prometheus/client_golang/promhttp
```

1. Modify your Go application to expose metrics.

File: `main.go`

go

```
package main

import (

    "fmt"

    "log"

    "net/http"

    "os"
```

```go
    "github.com/prometheus/client_golang/prometheus"

    "github.com/prometheus/client_golang/prometheus/promhttp"
)

var (

    // Define a new counter metric for HTTP requests

    httpRequests = prometheus.NewCounterVec(

        prometheus.CounterOpts{

            Name: "http_requests_total",

            Help: "Total number of HTTP requests.",

        },

        []string{"method", "status"},

    )

)

func init() {
```

```go
    // Register the metric with Prometheus

    prometheus.MustRegister(httpRequests)

}


func    handler(w    http.ResponseWriter,    r
*http.Request) {

    // Increment the counter on each request

    httpRequests.WithLabelValues(r.Method,
"200").Inc()


    // Simulate some work

    serverName := os.Getenv("SERVER_NAME")

    fmt.Fprintf(w,    "Hello    from    %s",
serverName)

}


func main() {

    // Register the HTTP handler

    http.HandleFunc("/", handler)
```

```go
    // Expose the Prometheus metrics on the
/metrics endpoint

    http.Handle("/metrics",
promhttp.Handler())


    // Start the HTTP server

    port := os.Getenv("PORT")

    if port == "" {

        port = "8080"

    }

    log.Printf("Server listening on port
%s", port)

    log.Fatal(http.ListenAndServe(":"+port,
nil))

}
```

In this example:

- We define a **counter metric** httpRequests to track the total number of HTTP requests, categorized by HTTP method and response status.

- The `/metrics` endpoint exposes the metrics in a format that Prometheus can scrape.

Step 3: Configure Prometheus to Scrape Your Application

Prometheus needs to know where to scrape metrics from. To do this, you need to configure Prometheus by editing the `prometheus.yml` file.

File: `prometheus.yml`

yaml

```
global:
  scrape_interval: 15s
scrape_configs:
  - job_name: 'go-web-app'
    static_configs:
      - targets: ['localhost:8080']
```

This configuration tells Prometheus to scrape metrics from your Go application every 15 seconds.

Step 4: Visualizing Metrics with Grafana

Once Prometheus is collecting metrics, you can visualize them using Grafana.

1. Create a new dashboard in Grafana.
2. Add a new data source and select Prometheus as the source.
3. Create a panel to visualize the `http_requests_total` metric, which will show the number of HTTP requests over time.

For more detailed instructions on using Grafana with Prometheus, refer to the Grafana documentation.

Setting Up Logging for Go Applications

Logging is equally important as monitoring. Logs provide a detailed record of what happens inside your application, which is invaluable for debugging and troubleshooting.

In Go, you can use the built-in `log` package for basic logging, but for more advanced features like structured logging, we recommend using a third-party library such as **Logrus** or **Zap**.

We will demonstrate logging using **Logrus**, a structured logger for Go.

Step 1: Install Logrus

Install Logrus by running the following command:

bash

```bash
go get github.com/sirupsen/logrus
```

Step 2: Add Logging to Your Application

Modify your Go application to log important events, such as incoming requests and errors.

File: main.go

go

```go
package main

import (

    "fmt"

    "log"

    "net/http"

    "os"

    "github.com/sirupsen/logrus"

)

var (

    logger = logrus.New()
```

```go
)

func init() {
    // Set the log format and output
    logger.SetFormatter(&logrus.JSONFormatter{})
    logger.SetOutput(os.Stdout)
}

func handler(w http.ResponseWriter, r *http.Request) {
    // Log the incoming request
    logger.WithFields(logrus.Fields{
        "method": r.Method,
        "uri":    r.RequestURI,
    }).Info("Received request")

    // Simulate some work
    serverName := os.Getenv("SERVER_NAME")
    fmt.Fprintf(w, "Hello from %s", serverName)
```

```go
}

func main() {

    // Register the HTTP handler

    http.HandleFunc("/", handler)


    // Start the HTTP server

    port := os.Getenv("PORT")

    if port == "" {

        port = "8080"

    }

    logger.Infof("Server listening on port
%s", port)

    log.Fatal(http.ListenAndServe(":"+port,
nil))

}
```

In this example:

- We use **Logrus** to log incoming requests, including the HTTP method and URI.

- Logs are formatted in JSON, which makes them easy to parse and analyze in a logging system.

Step 3: Centralized Logging with ELK Stack (Optional)

While logging locally can be useful, in a production environment, it's often better to centralize your logs. One popular solution is the **ELK Stack** (Elasticsearch, Logstash, and Kibana), which allows you to collect, store, and visualize logs.

To set up centralized logging with ELK:

1. Install Elasticsearch, Logstash, and Kibana.
2. Configure Logstash to collect logs from your Go application.
3. Use Kibana to visualize and search through your logs.

For more information on setting up the ELK stack, refer to the official documentation.

Best Practices for Monitoring and Logging

- **Use Structured Logging**: Structured logs (e.g., JSON format) make it easier to search and analyze logs.
- **Monitor Key Metrics**: Track important application metrics such as request rates, error rates, and response times.
- **Set Up Alerts**: Use monitoring tools to set up alerts for critical issues, such as high error rates or slow response times.

- **Log at Appropriate Levels**: Use different log levels (e.g., INFO, WARN, ERROR) to categorize logs based on severity.
- **Retain Logs**: Ensure that logs are retained for a reasonable period to help with troubleshooting and audits.

Hands-On Exercise: Deploy the task management application to a cloud platform using Docker.

In this hands-on exercise, we'll take the task management application we developed earlier and deploy it to a cloud platform using Docker. Docker allows us to containerize our application, making it easier to deploy and scale. By the end of this exercise, you will have a solid understanding of how to containerize an application and deploy it to a cloud platform.

Prerequisites

- Basic knowledge of Go programming.
- A task management application that we have built earlier in this book.
- Docker installed on your local machine. If you haven't installed Docker, you can follow the installation guide here.
- A cloud account (AWS, GCP, or Heroku). In this exercise, we'll focus on Heroku, but the principles apply to other cloud platforms as well.

Step 1: Containerizing the Task Management Application

Before deploying the application, we need to containerize it using Docker. This involves creating a Docker image that contains all the necessary dependencies to run our Go application.

1.1 Create a Dockerfile

The first step is to create a `Dockerfile` in the root directory of your project. The Dockerfile is a script that defines how the Docker image will be built.

Here is an example of a `Dockerfile` for a Go application:

dockerfile

```
# Step 1: Use the official Go image as a base
image

FROM golang:1.19-alpine as builder

# Step 2: Set the working directory inside
the container

WORKDIR /app

# Step 3: Copy the Go module files to the
container

COPY go.mod go.sum ./

# Step 4: Download the Go module dependencies
```

```
RUN go mod tidy


# Step 5: Copy the entire project to the
container

COPY . .


# Step 6: Build the Go application

RUN go build -o taskmanager .


# Step 7: Create a new image for the runtime
environment

FROM alpine:latest


# Step 8: Install dependencies for running
the Go binary

RUN apk --no-cache add ca-certificates


# Step 9: Copy the compiled binary from the
builder image
```

```
COPY     --from=builder    /app/taskmanager
/taskmanager
```

```
# Step 10: Expose the port that the app will
run on
```

```
EXPOSE 8080
```

```
# Step 11: Run the Go binary when the
container starts
```

```
CMD ["/taskmanager"]
```

Explanation of the Dockerfile:

1. **FROM golang:1.19-alpine**: This specifies the base image to use. We're using the official Go image based on Alpine Linux, which is lightweight and optimized for container environments.
2. **WORKDIR /app**: This sets the working directory inside the container where the application files will be placed.
3. **COPY go.mod go.sum ./**: This copies the Go module files to the container to handle dependencies.
4. **RUN go mod tidy**: This installs the dependencies defined in `go.mod`.

5. **COPY . .:** This copies the entire application code into the container.
6. **RUN go build -o taskmanager .:** This builds the Go application and creates a binary called `taskmanager`.
7. **FROM alpine:latest:** This creates a new image based on Alpine Linux for the runtime environment. This step helps to reduce the size of the final image by only including the necessary runtime components.
8. **RUN apk --no-cache add ca-certificates:** This installs certificates needed for secure HTTP connections.
9. **COPY --from=builder /app/taskmanager /taskmanager:** This copies the compiled binary from the build stage to the runtime stage.
10. **EXPOSE 8080:** This exposes port 8080 so the application can accept HTTP requests.
11. **CMD ["/taskmanager"]:** This runs the Go binary when the container starts.

Step 2: Building the Docker Image

With the `Dockerfile` created, the next step is to build the Docker image. Open a terminal and navigate to the root directory of your project (where the `Dockerfile` is located). Then, run the following command:

bash

```
docker build -t taskmanager .
```

Explanation:

- `docker build` tells Docker to build an image.
- `-t taskmanager` assigns the name `taskmanager` to the image.
- `.` specifies the current directory as the build context.

Docker will start building the image based on the instructions in the `Dockerfile`. Once the build is complete, you can verify that the image was created by running:

bash

```
docker images
```

You should see the `taskmanager` image listed.

Step 3: Running the Docker Container Locally

Now that we have a Docker image, we can run it locally to make sure everything works as expected.

Run the following command to start the container:

bash

```
docker run -p 8080:8080 taskmanager
```

Explanation:

- `docker run` starts a new container from the specified image.
- `-p 8080:8080` maps port 8080 on your local machine to port 8080 inside the container, allowing you to access the application via `http://localhost:8080`.
- `taskmanager` is the name of the Docker image.

Once the container is running, you can open a browser and navigate to `http://localhost:8080` to access your task management application.

Step 4: Deploying the Dockerized Application to Heroku

Now that our application is containerized and running locally, it's time to deploy it to a cloud platform. In this section, we will deploy the application to **Heroku**, a popular platform-as-a-service (PaaS) that supports Docker deployments.

4.1 Install the Heroku CLI

To interact with Heroku, you need to install the Heroku Command Line Interface (CLI). You can download and install it from the official website: Heroku CLI.

After installing, log in to your Heroku account:

bash

```
heroku login
```

4.2 Create a Heroku Application

Run the following command to create a new Heroku application:

bash

```
heroku create taskmanager-app
```

This will create a new Heroku app with the name `taskmanager-app`. If you want to specify a custom name, replace `taskmanager-app` with your desired name.

4.3 Add Heroku Container Registry

Heroku provides a container registry where we can push our Docker image. To set this up, run the following command:

bash

```
heroku container:login
```

This command authenticates Docker with the Heroku container registry.

4.4 Push the Docker Image to Heroku

Now that we're logged in to the Heroku container registry, we can push the Docker image. Run the following command:

bash

```
heroku container:push web --app taskmanager-app
```

Explanation:

- `heroku container:push web` pushes the Docker image to Heroku's container registry.
- `--app taskmanager-app` specifies the name of the Heroku app.

4.5 Release the Application on Heroku

Once the image is pushed, we need to release it on Heroku. Run the following command:

bash

```
heroku      container:release      web      --app
taskmanager-app
```

This will release the Docker container and make the application live on Heroku.

4.6 Open the Application in Your Browser

After releasing the application, you can open it in your browser by running:

bash

```
heroku open --app taskmanager-app
```

This will open the task management application hosted on Heroku.

Step 5: Scaling the Application

One of the key benefits of using Docker and cloud platforms is the ability to scale your application. With Heroku, scaling is easy. To scale your application, you can run multiple instances (dynos) of your app.

To scale your app to two dynos, run:

bash

```bash
heroku ps:scale web=2 --app taskmanager-app
```

This will start two instances of your application, improving its availability and handling more traffic.

Step 6: Monitoring and Logs

Heroku also provides built-in tools for monitoring and viewing logs.

To view the logs of your application, run:

bash

```bash
heroku logs --tail --app taskmanager-app
```

This will display real-time logs of your application, which is useful for debugging and monitoring.

Chapter 10: Complete Project: Building a Web Application

In this chapter, we will build a complete, end-to-end web application using Go. This project will combine everything we've learned so far: building a backend with Go, creating RESTful APIs, adding authentication, and deploying the application to production. We will build a **Blog or E-Commerce Application**, which will include basic features like user authentication, blog posts or products, and a simple frontend to display content.

By the end of this chapter, you will have a fully functional web application, ready to be deployed to production.

10.1 Project Overview: A Blog or E-Commerce Application

In this chapter, we will guide you through building a complete web application using Go. The project will be a **Blog or E-Commerce Application**, where we will cover all the key steps in creating a functional backend, integrating essential features like user authentication, adding real-time capabilities, and deploying the application to production.

By the end of this chapter, you will have a fully functional web application that you can customize and extend to meet your needs. Whether you choose to build a blog or an e-commerce platform, the

498

steps and principles we'll follow are highly transferable to a wide range of web applications.

Let's start by discussing the two options for the project: **Blog Application** and **E-Commerce Application**.

Option 1: Blog Application

A blog application is a content-driven platform where users can create, read, update, and delete posts. This is a great choice for learning how to manage content dynamically, handle user authentication, and display data in a user-friendly format.

Features of the Blog Application:

1. **User Authentication:**
   ○ Users can sign up and log in to post content.
   ○ Authentication ensures that only authorized users can create or modify posts.
2. **CRUD Operations for Posts:**
   ○ Users can create new posts, edit existing ones, and delete them.
   ○ Each post will have a title, content, and author.
3. **Viewing Posts:**
   ○ Visitors to the site can read the posts but cannot modify them unless they are logged in.
4. **Comments (Optional):**

○ Users can leave comments on posts. This feature can be added later to make the blog more interactive.

Tech Stack for the Blog Application:

- **Backend:** Go (Golang)
- **Frontend:** HTML templates (for simplicity)
- **Authentication:** Sessions for managing user logins
- **Database:** In-memory storage or a lightweight database like SQLite for storing posts and user information
- **Real-time Features (Optional):** WebSockets for live notifications when a new post is created or when a comment is made

---

Option 2: E-Commerce Application

An e-commerce application allows users to browse products, add them to a shopping cart, and make purchases. This option is slightly more complex but will give you valuable experience in handling transactions, user sessions, and scaling.

Features of the E-Commerce Application:

1. **Product Listings:**
   ○ Products will be displayed on the homepage with images, descriptions, and prices.
2. **Shopping Cart:**
   ○ Users can add products to their shopping cart.

- The cart will keep track of the products, quantities, and total price.

3. **User Authentication:**
   - Users must sign up and log in to make a purchase.

4. **Checkout Process:**
   - Users can proceed to checkout, where they can review their order and confirm the purchase.

5. **Order History:**
   - After completing a purchase, users can view their order history.

Tech Stack for the E-Commerce Application:

- **Backend:** Go (Golang)
- **Frontend:** HTML templates or a simple frontend framework like Bootstrap for styling
- **Authentication:** Sessions for managing user logins
- **Database:** A relational database like PostgreSQL or MySQL for storing products, user data, and orders
- **Payment Integration (Optional):** You can integrate a service like Stripe for handling payments

---

Key Concepts Covered in This Chapter

No matter which application you choose, the following key concepts will be covered in this chapter:

1. **Setting Up the Backend:**

- We will begin by setting up the Go backend for the application. This includes defining the project structure, initializing Go modules, and setting up basic routing.

2. **Building RESTful APIs:**
   - We will create the necessary RESTful APIs for managing posts or products, and handle CRUD operations.

3. **Creating Dynamic Templates:**
   - We will use Go's `html/template` package to create dynamic HTML templates that display posts or products and allow users to interact with the application.

4. **Authentication:**
   - We will implement user authentication using sessions, allowing users to log in, create content, and interact with the application securely.

5. **Real-Time Features (Optional):**
   - We will demonstrate how to add real-time features to the application using WebSockets, such as live notifications when a new post is created or when a comment is added.

6. **Deployment:**
   - We will walk through the process of deploying the application to a cloud platform, such as Heroku or AWS, using Docker.

How This Chapter Will Help You

- **Hands-on Experience:** By building a complete application from scratch, you will gain valuable experience in full-stack web development.
- **Real-World Application:** The skills you learn in this chapter are highly applicable to real-world projects, whether you're building a blog, an e-commerce site, or any other web application.
- **Clear, Step-by-Step Approach:** This chapter is designed to be approachable for both beginners and experts. Each step is explained clearly with well-commented code examples, so you can follow along and understand how everything works.

Next Steps

In the following sections of this chapter, we will:

1. Set up the Go backend for the application.
2. Build RESTful APIs for managing posts or products.
3. Implement user authentication to secure the application.
4. Add dynamic templates to display content.
5. Optionally, integrate real-time features and deploy the application to a cloud platform.

By the end of this chapter, you will have a complete web application that is ready to be deployed and used in production.

10.2 Setting Up the Backend with Go

In this section, we'll set up the backend for our web application using Go (Golang). This will include defining the project structure, initializing Go modules, and setting up basic routing to handle HTTP requests. Whether you're building a blog or an e-commerce platform, the steps we'll take here are fundamental to any web application.

We'll walk through the process step-by-step, ensuring that even beginners can follow along, while also providing enough depth for more experienced developers to appreciate the concepts and best practices.

Step 1: Initialize Your Go Project

Before we start coding, let's initialize a Go project. This will create a module and set up the necessary files for Go to manage your dependencies.

1.1 Create a Project Directory

Start by creating a directory for your project. You can name it based on the type of application you're building (e.g., `blog-app` or `ecommerce-app`).

bash

```
mkdir blog-app
cd blog-app
```

1.2 Initialize Go Module

Next, initialize the Go module. This will create a `go.mod` file that tracks your dependencies.

bash

```
go mod init blog-app
```

The `go.mod` file is essential for Go's dependency management. It keeps track of the version of Go you are using, as well as any external libraries or packages that you might need.

Step 2: Set Up the Basic Project Structure

Now, let's organize the project files. Here's a simple structure for your backend:

go

```
blog-app/
```

```
├── main.go
├── handlers/
│   └── post.go
├── models/
│   └── post.go
├── templates/
│   └── index.html
└── go.mod
```

- **main.go:** This will be the entry point for your application. It will set up the server and routing.
- **handlers/post.go:** This will contain the logic for handling HTTP requests related to blog posts (e.g., creating, viewing, updating, and deleting posts).
- **models/post.go:** This will define the structure for a blog post and any database-related logic.
- **templates/index.html:** This will be the HTML template for rendering the posts.

Step 3: Set Up the Web Server and Routing

Let's start by writing the basic code to set up the web server and routing. We'll use Go's built-in `net/http` package for this.

3.1 Create `main.go`

In `main.go`, we will initialize the web server and define the routes.

go

```go
package main

import (

    "blog-app/handlers"

    "log"

    "net/http"

)


func main() {

    // Set up routes

    http.HandleFunc("/", handlers.HomePage)

    http.HandleFunc("/create",
handlers.CreatePost)
```

```go
    http.HandleFunc("/view",
handlers.ViewPost)

    // Start the server

    log.Println("Starting      server      on
:8080...")

    err := http.ListenAndServe(":8080", nil)

    if err != nil {

        log.Fatal("Error starting server: ",
err)

    }

}
```

- **http.HandleFunc("/", handlers.HomePage):** This sets up the route for the homepage, which will display the list of posts.
- **http.HandleFunc("/create", handlers.CreatePost):** This route will handle creating new posts.
- **http.HandleFunc("/view", handlers.ViewPost):** This route will handle viewing individual posts.

3.2 Create the Handlers

Next, let's create the handlers for each route. In the `handlers/post.go` file, we'll define the logic for rendering the homepage and handling post creation.

```go
package handlers

import (

    "blog-app/models"

    "html/template"

    "net/http"

)

// HomePage renders the homepage with a list
of posts

func HomePage(w    http.ResponseWriter,    r
*http.Request) {

    // Simulate fetching posts from the
database

    posts := []models.Post{

        {Title: "First Post", Content: "This
is the first post."},
```

```go
        {Title: "Second Post", Content:
"This is the second post."},

    }

    // Parse the template
    tmpl, err :=
template.ParseFiles("templates/index.html")
    if err != nil {
        http.Error(w, err.Error(),
http.StatusInternalServerError)
        return
    }
    // Execute the template and pass the
posts to it
    err = tmpl.Execute(w, posts)
    if err != nil {
        http.Error(w, err.Error(),
http.StatusInternalServerError)
    }
```

```go
}

// CreatePost renders the form for creating a
new post

func CreatePost(w http.ResponseWriter, r
*http.Request) {

    if r.Method == http.MethodPost {

        // Handle form submission

        title := r.FormValue("title")

        content := r.FormValue("content")


        // Simulate saving the post to the
database

        // In a real application, you would
save this to a database

        newPost := models.Post{Title: title,
Content: content}


        // Redirect to the homepage after
creating the post
```

```
        http.Redirect(w,          r,          "/",
http.StatusSeeOther)

        return

    }

    // Render the form for creating a post

    http.ServeFile(w,                            r,
"templates/create_post.html")

}
```

- **HomePage:** This function simulates fetching posts from a database (we'll use static data for now) and renders them using an HTML template.
- **CreatePost:** This function handles the form submission for creating a new post. It reads the title and content from the form, simulates saving it, and redirects to the homepage.

Step 4: Create Templates for Displaying Content

Now let's create the HTML templates to display the content. We'll start with the homepage template (`templates/index.html`).

4.1 Create `templates/index.html`

This template will display the list of posts.

html

```html
<!DOCTYPE html>

<html lang="en">

<head>

    <meta charset="UTF-8">

    <meta                         name="viewport"
content="width=device-width,          initial-
scale=1.0">

    <title>Blog</title>

</head>

<body>

    <h1>Blog Posts</h1>

    <ul>

        {{range .}}

            <li>

                <h2>{{.Title}}</h2>

                <p>{{.Content}}</p>
```

```
      </li>

    {{end}}

  </ul>

  <a href="/create">Create New Post</a>

</body>

</html>
```

- **{{range .}}**: This Go template action loops through the posts passed to the template and displays each post's title and content.

4.2 Create `templates/create_post.html`

This template will display the form for creating a new post.

html

```
<!DOCTYPE html>

<html lang="en">

<head>

    <meta charset="UTF-8">
```

```html
    <meta                      name="viewport"
content="width=device-width,        initial-
scale=1.0">

    <title>Create New Post</title>

</head>

<body>

    <h1>Create New Post</h1>

    <form action="/create" method="post">

        <label for="title">Title:</label>

        <input    type="text"    id="title"
name="title" required><br><br>

        <label
for="content">Content:</label>

        <textarea              id="content"
name="content" required></textarea><br><br>

        <button
type="submit">Submit</button>

    </form>

    <a href="/">Back to Posts</a>

</body>
```

```
</html>
```

- This form allows users to enter the title and content for a new post. When the form is submitted, it sends a POST request to the /create route.

Step 5: Run the Application

Now that we've set up the basic structure, let's run the application.

In the terminal, navigate to your project directory and run:

bash

```
go run main.go
```

You should see the message Starting server on :8080... in the terminal. Open your browser and go to http://localhost:8080 to view the homepage.

10.3 Building RESTful APIs and Dynamic Templates

In this chapter, we will focus on building RESTful APIs to handle the backend logic of our web application and use Go's `html/template` package to create dynamic templates for the frontend. By the end of this chapter, you will have a clear understanding of how to integrate APIs with templates, making your application interactive and user-friendly.

Learning Objectives

- Understand the principles of RESTful API design.
- Build and integrate RESTful APIs using Go.
- Use Go's `html/template` package to create dynamic HTML pages.
- Combine backend logic and frontend templates to deliver a seamless user experience.

---

1. Understanding RESTful APIs

RESTful APIs provide a standardized way for applications to communicate. They use HTTP methods such as:

- **GET**: Retrieve data.
- **POST**: Create new data.
- **PUT**: Update existing data.
- **DELETE**: Remove data.

Example: Blog Application

In a blog application, you might have the following RESTful API endpoints:

- GET /posts: Retrieve all blog posts.
- POST /posts: Create a new blog post.
- GET /posts/{id}: Retrieve a specific blog post.
- PUT /posts/{id}: Update a specific blog post.
- DELETE /posts/{id}: Delete a specific blog post.

---

2. Building RESTful APIs in Go

Go's net/http package is ideal for building RESTful APIs. Let's start by creating APIs for managing blog posts.

2.1 Project Structure

Organize the project as follows:

go

```
blog-app/

├── main.go

├── handlers/

│   ├── posts.go
```

```
├── models/
│   ├── post.go
├── templates/
│   ├── index.html
│   ├── post.html
└── go.mod
```

2.2 Define the Data Model

Create a Post struct in models/post.go:

go

```go
package models

// Post represents a blog post
type Post struct {
    ID      int    `json:"id"`
    Title   string `json:"title"`
    Content string `json:"content"`
```

```
}
```

2.3 Create API Handlers

In `handlers/posts.go`, define the API endpoints:

go

```go
package handlers

import (

    "encoding/json"

    "net/http"

    "strconv"

    "sync"

    "blog-app/models"

)

var (

    posts []models.Post

    idCounter int
```

```go
    mu sync.Mutex

)


// GetPosts retrieves all posts

func GetPosts(w http.ResponseWriter, r *http.Request) {

    w.Header().Set("Content-Type", "application/json")

    json.NewEncoder(w).Encode(posts)

}


// CreatePost adds a new post

func CreatePost(w http.ResponseWriter, r *http.Request) {

    var post models.Post

    if err := json.NewDecoder(r.Body).Decode(&post); err != nil {

        http.Error(w, "Invalid input", http.StatusBadRequest)
```

```go
        return
    }

    mu.Lock()

    idCounter++

    post.ID = idCounter

    posts = append(posts, post)

    mu.Unlock()


    w.Header().Set("Content-Type",
"application/json")

    json.NewEncoder(w).Encode(post)
}


// GetPost retrieves a single post by ID

func    GetPost(w    http.ResponseWriter,    r
*http.Request) {

    idStr := r.URL.Query().Get("id")

    id, err := strconv.Atoi(idStr)
```

```go
    if err != nil {
        http.Error(w,        "Invalid        ID",
http.StatusBadRequest)
        return
    }


    for _, post := range posts {
        if post.ID == id {
            w.Header().Set("Content-Type",
"application/json")
            json.NewEncoder(w).Encode(post)
            return
        }
    }


    http.Error(w,    "Post    not    found",
http.StatusNotFound)
}
```

3. Creating Dynamic Templates

Dynamic templates enable the rendering of HTML pages with data passed from the backend.

3.1 HTML Templates

Create `templates/index.html`:

html

```
<!DOCTYPE html>

<html>

<head>

    <title>Blog</title>

</head>

<body>

    <h1>Blog Posts</h1>

    <ul>

        {{range .}}

        <li>

            <h2>{{.Title}}</h2>

            <p>{{.Content}}</p>
```

```
        </li>

        {{end}}

    </ul>

</body>

</html>
```

3.2 Template Rendering

In `handlers/posts.go`, add a function to render the template:

go

```go
package handlers


import (

    "html/template"

    "net/http"

)

// RenderPosts renders the blog posts on the
homepage
```

```go
func RenderPosts(w http.ResponseWriter, r *http.Request) {

    tmpl, err := template.ParseFiles("templates/index.html")

    if err != nil {

        http.Error(w, "Template parsing error", http.StatusInternalServerError)

        return

    }


    tmpl.Execute(w, posts)

}
```

---

4. Integrating APIs and Templates

In main.go, set up routes for the APIs and the homepage:

go

```go
package main

import (

    "log"
```

```go
    "net/http"

    "blog-app/handlers"
)

func main() {

    http.HandleFunc("/api/posts",
handlers.GetPosts)

    http.HandleFunc("/api/posts/create",
handlers.CreatePost)

    http.HandleFunc("/",
handlers.RenderPosts)


    log.Println("Server        running        on
http://localhost:8080")

    log.Fatal(http.ListenAndServe(":8080",
nil))

}
```

---

5. Testing the Application

1. **Run the Server:** Start the server using `go run main.go`.

Create a Post: Use a tool like Postman or `curl` to send a POST request:

bash

```
curl -X POST -H "Content-Type:
application/json" -d '{"title":"First
Post","content":"This is the first post."}'
http://localhost:8080/api/posts/create
```

2.
3. **View Posts:** Open `http://localhost:8080` in your browser to see the rendered posts.

---

6. Enhancements

- **Add Pagination:** Modify the `GetPosts` handler to support pagination.
- **Include CSS:** Enhance the HTML templates with CSS for better styling.
- **Add Error Handling:** Improve error handling for invalid inputs or server issues.

10.4 Adding Authentication and Real-Time Features

In this chapter, we will enhance our web application by adding user authentication and real-time features. Authentication will secure parts of the application, ensuring only authorized users can access certain functionalities. Real-time features will make the application more dynamic, enabling live updates without refreshing the page.

Learning Objectives

- Understand the basics of user authentication.
- Implement user login, registration, and session management.
- Add real-time features using WebSockets for live interactions.
- Integrate authentication and real-time updates into the existing application.

---

1. Adding User Authentication

Authentication ensures that users can securely log in and access personalized features.

1.1 Setting Up User Models

Create a User struct in models/user.go:

go

```go
package models

// User represents an application user

type User struct {
```

```go
    ID       int    `json:"id"`

    Username string `json:"username"`

    Password string `json:"password"`

}
```

1.2 Hashing Passwords

Use Go's `bcrypt` package to hash passwords securely. Install the package:

bash

```bash
go get golang.org/x/crypto/bcrypt
```

Add a utility function in `models/user.go`:

go

```go
package models

import (

    "golang.org/x/crypto/bcrypt"

)

// HashPassword hashes a plaintext password
```

```go
func HashPassword(password string) (string,
error) {

    hashed,            err            :=
bcrypt.GenerateFromPassword([]byte(password)
, bcrypt.DefaultCost)

    return string(hashed), err

}

// CheckPassword verifies a plaintext
password against a hashed password
func CheckPassword(hashedPassword, password
string) error {

    return
bcrypt.CompareHashAndPassword([]byte(hashedP
assword), []byte(password))

}
```

1.3 User Registration

Create a handler for user registration in handlers/auth.go:

go

```go
package handlers
```

```go
import (

    "encoding/json"

    "net/http"

    "sync"

    "blog-app/models"

)

var (

    users      []models.User

    userID     int

    userMutex  sync.Mutex

)

// RegisterUser registers a new user

func RegisterUser(w http.ResponseWriter, r
*http.Request) {

    var user models.User

    if                    err                    :=
json.NewDecoder(r.Body).Decode(&user);    err
!= nil {
```

```go
        http.Error(w,       "Invalid     input",
http.StatusBadRequest)

        return

    }

    hashedPassword,                err             :=
models.HashPassword(user.Password)

    if err != nil {

        http.Error(w,       "Error       hashing
password", http.StatusInternalServerError)

        return

    }


    userMutex.Lock()

    userID++

    user.ID = userID

    user.Password = hashedPassword

    users = append(users, user)

    userMutex.Unlock()
```

```go
    w.WriteHeader(http.StatusCreated)

    json.NewEncoder(w).Encode(map[string]string{
    "message": "User registered successfully"})

}
```

1.4 User Login

Add a login handler in handlers/auth.go:

go

```go
// LoginUser authenticates a user

func LoginUser(w http.ResponseWriter, r
*http.Request) {

    var credentials struct {

        Username string `json:"username"`

        Password string `json:"password"`

    }

    if err :=
json.NewDecoder(r.Body).Decode(&credentials)
; err != nil {
```

```go
        http.Error(w,     "Invalid     input",
http.StatusBadRequest)

        return

    }

    for _, user := range users {

        if          user.Username          ==
credentials.Username {

            if                err              :=
models.CheckPassword(user.Password,
credentials.Password); err == nil {

                http.SetCookie(w,
&http.Cookie{

                    Name:   "session_token",

                    Value:   "authenticated",
// Simplified for demonstration

                    Path:   "/",

                })

                w.WriteHeader(http.StatusOK)
```

```go
json.NewEncoder(w).Encode(map[string]string{
"message": "Login successful"})

            return

        }

    }

}

    http.Error(w,    "Invalid    username    or
password", http.StatusUnauthorized)

}
```

---

2. Adding Real-Time Features

Real-time updates improve user experience by enabling live interactions.

2.1 Setting Up WebSockets

Install the `gorilla/websocket` package:

bash

```bash
go get github.com/gorilla/websocket
```

2.2 WebSocket Handlers

Add a WebSocket handler in `handlers/realtime.go`:

go

```go
package handlers

import (

    "net/http"

    "github.com/gorilla/websocket"

)

var upgrader = websocket.Upgrader{

    CheckOrigin: func(r *http.Request) bool {

        return true

    },

}

var                 connections                 =
make(map[*websocket.Conn]bool)
```

```go
// HandleWebSocket manages WebSocket
connections
func HandleWebSocket(w http.ResponseWriter, r
*http.Request) {

    conn, err := upgrader.Upgrade(w, r, nil)

    if err != nil {

        http.Error(w, "Failed to upgrade
connection", http.StatusInternalServerError)

        return

    }

    defer conn.Close()


    connections[conn] = true

    for {

        var message map[string]string

        if err := conn.ReadJSON(&message);
err != nil {

            delete(connections, conn)

            break
```

```go
        }

        for c := range connections {
                if err := c.WriteJSON(message);
err != nil {
                        delete(connections, c)
                }
        }
    }
}
```

2.3 Frontend Integration

Add a WebSocket client in `templates/index.html`:

html

```html
<script>
    const        socket        =        new
WebSocket("ws://localhost:8080/ws");

    socket.onmessage = function(event) {
        const data = JSON.parse(event.data);
```

```javascript
      const           messageList           =
document.getElementById("messages");

      const           newMessage           =
document.createElement("li");

      newMessage.textContent           =
`${data.user}: ${data.message}`;

      messageList.appendChild(newMessage);

    };

    function sendMessage() {

      const             user           =
document.getElementById("user").value;

      const           message           =
document.getElementById("message").value;

      socket.send(JSON.stringify({   user,
message }));

    }

</script>
```

---

3. Integrating Authentication and Real-Time Features

Secure WebSocket connections by checking user authentication in `HandleWebSocket`:

go

```go
cookie, err := r.Cookie("session_token")

if err != nil || cookie.Value != "authenticated" {

    http.Error(w, "Unauthorized", http.StatusUnauthorized)

    return

}
```

---

4. Testing the Features

1. **Run the Server:** Start the server with `go run main.go`.
2. **Register Users:** Use Postman or `curl` to register and log in users.
3. **Test WebSockets:** Open the application in multiple browser tabs to send and receive real-time messages.

10.5 Deployment and Testing

Deploying and testing are the final steps to ensure your web application is production-ready. Deployment makes your application accessible to users, while testing ensures it performs as expected under various conditions. This chapter will guide you through deploying the complete application and conducting thorough testing.

Learning Objectives

- Understand deployment workflows for Go applications.
- Deploy the application to a cloud platform.
- Test the application for functionality, performance, and security.
- Use automation tools to streamline testing and deployment.

1. Preparing for Deployment

1.1 Configuring Environment Variables

Environment variables are critical for storing sensitive information like database credentials and API keys. Use a `.env` file and the `godotenv` package:

Install the package:

bash

```
go get github.com/joho/godotenv
```

Load the .env file in main.go:

go

```go
package main

import (

    "log"

    "os"


    "github.com/joho/godotenv"

)


func init() {

    if err := godotenv.Load(); err != nil {

        log.Println("No .env file found")

    }
```

```go
}

func main() {

    port := os.Getenv("PORT")

    if port == "" {

        port = "8080"

    }

    log.Printf("Server starting on port %s",
port)

}
```

Create a .env file:

makefile

```
PORT=8080

DATABASE_URL=your_database_connection_string
```

1.2 Building the Application

Compile the Go application into an executable binary:

bash

```
go build -o app .
```

---

2. Deploying to a Cloud Platform

2.1 Using Docker for Deployment

Docker simplifies deployment by packaging the application and its dependencies into a container.

1. **Create a** `Dockerfile`:

dockerfile

```
# Use an official Go image as a base

FROM golang:1.20-alpine

# Set the working directory

WORKDIR /app

# Copy the Go module files and download
dependencies

COPY go.mod go.sum ./

RUN go mod download
```

```
# Copy the application source code

COPY . .


# Build the application

RUN go build -o main .


# Expose the application port

EXPOSE 8080


# Run the application

CMD ["./main"]
```

2. **Build the Docker image:**

bash

```
docker build -t my-go-app .
```

3. **Run the container locally to test:**

bash

```
docker run -p 8080:8080 --env-file .env my-go-app
```

2.2 Deploying to AWS

1. **Push the Docker Image to Amazon Elastic Container Registry (ECR):**

bash

```
aws ecr create-repository --repository-name my-go-app

aws ecr get-login-password --region your-region | docker login --username AWS --password-stdin <your-account-id>.dkr.ecr.your-region.amazonaws.com

docker tag my-go-app:latest <your-account-id>.dkr.ecr.your-region.amazonaws.com/my-go-app:latest

docker push <your-account-id>.dkr.ecr.your-region.amazonaws.com/my-go-app:latest
```

2. **Deploy the Image to Amazon Elastic Kubernetes Service (EKS):**

- Set up an EKS cluster.
- Deploy the application using a Kubernetes deployment file.

---

3. Testing the Application

3.1 Functional Testing

Functional testing ensures the application works as expected.

1. **Test APIs with Postman:**
   - Create test cases for all API endpoints.
   - Validate the response codes, payloads, and headers.
2. **Automate API Testing with `go test`:**

go

```go
package main

import (

    "net/http"

    "testing"

)

func TestHomePage(t *testing.T) {
```

```go
    resp,                    err                        :=
http.Get("http://localhost:8080/")

    if err != nil {

        t.Fatalf("Failed  to  send  request:
%v", err)

    }

    if resp.StatusCode != http.StatusOK {

        t.Errorf("Expected  status  OK,  got
%v", resp.Status)

    }

}
```

Run the tests:

bash

```
go test ./...
```

3.2 Performance Testing

Use tools like Apache JMeter or wrk to simulate high traffic and measure response times.

Example with `wrk`:

bash

```
wrk -t12 -c400 -d30s http://localhost:8080/
```

3.3 Security Testing

Check for vulnerabilities using tools like `gosec`:

Install `gosec`:

bash

```
go                    install
github.com/securego/gosec/v2/cmd/gosec@lates
t
```

Run a security scan:

bash

```
gosec ./...
```

---

4. Automating Deployment and Testing

4.1 Using GitHub Actions

Automate the build, test, and deployment process with GitHub Actions.

1. **Create a** `.github/workflows/deploy.yml` **file:**

yaml

```
name: Deploy to AWS

on:

  push:

    branches:

      - main


jobs:

  build-and-deploy:

    runs-on: ubuntu-latest


    steps:

    - name: Checkout code

      uses: actions/checkout@v3
```

```yaml
    - name: Set up Go

      uses: actions/setup-go@v4

      with:

        go-version: 1.20


    - name: Install dependencies

      run: go mod tidy


    - name: Run tests

      run: go test ./...


    - name: Build Docker image

      run: docker build -t my-go-app .


    - name: Push Docker image to ECR

      env:

        AWS_ACCESS_KEY_ID:                    ${{
  secrets.AWS_ACCESS_KEY_ID }}
```

```
    AWS_SECRET_ACCESS_KEY:              ${{
secrets.AWS_SECRET_ACCESS_KEY }}

    run: |

    aws ecr get-login-password --region
your-region | docker login --username AWS --
password-stdin              <your-account-
id>.dkr.ecr.your-region.amazonaws.com

    docker tag my-go-app:latest <your-
account-id>.dkr.ecr.your-
region.amazonaws.com/my-go-app:latest

    docker      push      <your-account-
id>.dkr.ecr.your-region.amazonaws.com/my-go-
app:latest
```

Final Hands-On Project: Develop a complete, end-to-end web application and deploy it to production.

Overview

This chapter is the culmination of everything you've learned so far. You'll build a fully functional, production-ready web application from scratch and deploy it to the cloud. We'll use a **blog application** as our project, which includes user authentication, a RESTful API, dynamic templates, and real-time features. Finally, we'll deploy the application using **Docker** to a cloud platform.

Learning Objectives

- Build a complete web application using Go.
- Implement user authentication and authorization.
- Create RESTful APIs and dynamic templates.
- Add real-time features using WebSockets.
- Deploy the application to a cloud platform with Docker.

---

1. Project Requirements

1.1 Prerequisites

Before starting, ensure you have the following installed:

- **Go** (1.20 or later)
- **Docker**
- **PostgreSQL** (or any other SQL database)
- A cloud platform account (AWS, GCP, or Heroku)

1.2 Project Structure

Organize the project with the following structure:

go

```
blog-app/
```

```
├── cmd/
│   └── main.go
├── internal/
│   ├── auth/
│   │   ├── auth.go
│   │   └── middleware.go
│   ├── models/
│   │   └── models.go
│   ├── posts/
│   │   └── posts.go
│   ├── templates/
│   │   ├── index.html
│   │   ├── login.html
│   │   └── post.html
```

├── Dockerfile

├── go.mod

└── .env

---

2. Setting Up the Backend

2.1 Initializing the Project

Create the project directory:
bash

```
mkdir blog-app && cd blog-app
```

Initialize the Go module:
bash

```
go mod init blog-app
```

Install required packages:
bash

```
go get github.com/gin-gonic/gin
```

```
go get github.com/jmoiron/sqlx

go get github.com/dgrijalva/jwt-go

go get github.com/joho/godotenv
```

2.2 Connecting to the Database

Create a `.env` file to store environment variables:
bash

```
DB_URL=postgres://username:password@localhos
t:5432/blogdb?sslmode=disable

JWT_SECRET=your_jwt_secret
```

Load the environment variables in `main.go`:
go

```
package main

import (

    "log"

    "os"
```

```go
        "github.com/gin-gonic/gin"

        "github.com/joho/godotenv"

        "github.com/jmoiron/sqlx"

)

var db *sqlx.DB

func init() {

        if err := godotenv.Load(); err != nil {

                log.Fatal("Error loading .env file")

        }


        var err error

        db, err = sqlx.Connect("postgres",
os.Getenv("DB_URL"))

        if err != nil {

                log.Fatal(err)

        }

}
```

```go
func main() {

    r := gin.Default()

    r.GET("/", func(c *gin.Context) {

        c.JSON(200,           gin.H{"message":
"Welcome to the Blog App!"})

    })

    r.Run(":8080")

}
```

---

3. Implementing Core Features

3.1 User Authentication

Create `auth.go` for handling JWT-based authentication:
go

```go
package auth

import (

    "time"


    "github.com/dgrijalva/jwt-go"
```

```go
)

var jwtKey = []byte("your_jwt_secret")

type Claims struct {

    Username string `json:"username"`

    jwt.StandardClaims

}

func GenerateToken(username string) (string,
error) {

    expirationTime := time.Now().Add(24 *
time.Hour)

    claims := &Claims{

        Username: username,

        StandardClaims: jwt.StandardClaims{

            ExpiresAt:
expirationTime.Unix(),

        },

    }
```

```go
    token                          :=
jwt.NewWithClaims(jwt.SigningMethodHS256,
claims)

    return token.SignedString(jwtKey)

}
```

Create middleware for authentication:

go

```go
package auth

import (

    "net/http"

    "github.com/gin-gonic/gin"

)


func AuthMiddleware() gin.HandlerFunc {

    return func(c *gin.Context) {

        tokenString                    :=
c.GetHeader("Authorization")

        if tokenString == "" {
```

```go
        c.JSON(http.StatusUnauthorized,
gin.H{"error": "Missing token"})

        c.Abort()

        return

    }


    claims := &Claims{}

    token,                    err                 :=
jwt.ParseWithClaims(tokenString,    claims,
func(token *jwt.Token) (interface{}, error) {

        return jwtKey, nil

    })

    if err != nil || !token.Valid {

        c.JSON(http.StatusUnauthorized,
gin.H{"error": "Invalid token"})

        c.Abort()

        return

    }
```

```go
        c.Set("username", claims.Username)

        c.Next()

    }

}
```

3.2 RESTful API for Blog Posts

Define the `Post` model in `models.go`:

go

```go
package models

type Post struct {

    ID       int     `db:"id"`

    Title    string `db:"title"`

    Content string `db:"content"`

    Author   string `db:"author"`

}
```

Create `posts.go` for handling posts:

go

```go
package posts

import (

    "net/http"

    "github.com/gin-gonic/gin"

)

func GetPosts(c *gin.Context) {

    // Fetch posts from the database (mocked
for now)

    posts := []map[string]string{

        {"title": "First Post", "content":
"This is the first post."},

    }

    c.JSON(http.StatusOK, posts)

}
```

Add routes in `main.go`:

go

```go
r.GET("/posts", posts.GetPosts)
```

---

4. Adding Real-Time Features

Add WebSocket support for real-time comments:
go

```go
package main

import (

    "github.com/gin-gonic/gin"

    "github.com/gorilla/websocket"

)

var upgrader = websocket.Upgrader{}

func handleWebSocket(c *gin.Context) {

    conn, err := upgrader.Upgrade(c.Writer,
c.Request, nil)

    if err != nil {

        return

    }
```

```go
    defer conn.Close()

    for {

        _, message, err := conn.ReadMessage()

        if err != nil {

            break

        }
conn.WriteMessage(websocket.TextMessage,
message)

    }

}

func main() {

    r.GET("/ws", handleWebSocket)

}
```

---

5. Deployment

Create a `Dockerfile`:
dockerfile

```dockerfile
FROM golang:1.20-alpine
```

```
WORKDIR /app

COPY . .

RUN go build -o main .

EXPOSE 8080

CMD ["./main"]
```

1. **Deploy to Heroku:**
   o   Install Heroku CLI.

Create a Heroku app:
bash

```
heroku create
```

Push the Docker image:
bash

```
heroku container:push web

heroku container:release web
```

---

6. Testing the Application

- Test the APIs using Postman.

- Perform load testing using `wrk`.

Appendices

Appendix A: Quick Reference for Go Syntax

This appendix provides a concise yet comprehensive overview of Go syntax. Whether you're a beginner or an experienced developer, this guide will help you quickly recall key concepts and features of the Go programming language.

1. Basic Syntax and Structure

Hello, World! Program

Every Go program starts with the `main` package and a `main()` function.

go

```go
package main

import "fmt"

func main() {
    fmt.Println("Hello, World!")
}
```

Explanation:

- `package main`: Defines the entry point of the program.
- `import "fmt"`: Imports the fmt package for formatted I/O.
- `func main()`: The main function where execution begins.

---

2. Variables and Constants

Declaring Variables

Go supports both explicit and implicit variable declarations.

go

```
// Explicit declaration

var name string = "Go"

// Implicit declaration (type inferred)

age := 10
```

Constants

Constants are immutable values defined using the `const` keyword.

go

```
const Pi = 3.14
```

3. Data Types

Go has several basic data types, including integers, floats, strings, and booleans.

Type	Description	Example
`int`, `uint`	Integer types	`var x int = 42`
`float32`	Floating-point types	`var y float32`
`string`	Text data	`var s string`
`bool`	Boolean values	`var b bool = true`

4. Control Structures

Conditional Statements

go

```go
if x := 10; x > 5 {
    fmt.Println("x is greater than 5")
} else {
    fmt.Println("x is less than or equal to 5")
}
```

Loops

The for loop is the only looping construct in Go.

go

```go
for i := 0; i < 5; i++ {
    fmt.Println(i)
}
```

Switch Statements

go

```go
switch day := "Monday"; day {
case "Monday":
```

```go
        fmt.Println("Start of the week")
default:
        fmt.Println("Another day")
}
```

---

5. Functions

Defining and Calling Functions

go

```go
func add(a int, b int) int {
        return a + b
}
result := add(3, 4)
fmt.Println("Sum:", result)
```

Variadic Functions

go

```go
func sum(nums ...int) int {
```

```go
    total := 0

    for _, num := range nums {

        total += num

    }

    return total

}

fmt.Println(sum(1, 2, 3, 4)) // Output: 10
```

---

6. Data Structures

Arrays and Slices

Arrays: Fixed-size collection.
go
```go
arr := [3]int{1, 2, 3}
```

Slices: Dynamic-size collection.
go
```go
slice := []int{1, 2, 3}

slice = append(slice, 4)
```

Maps

Maps are key-value pairs.

go

```go
m := map[string]int{"one": 1, "two": 2}
fmt.Println(m["one"]) // Output: 1
```

Structs

Structs group related data.

go

```go
type Person struct {
    Name string
    Age  int
}
p := Person{Name: "Alice", Age: 25}
fmt.Println(p.Name) // Output: Alice
```

---

7. Pointers

Pointers hold memory addresses.

```go
x := 42

p := &x // Pointer to x

fmt.Println(*p) // Dereference to get value: 42
```

---

8. Concurrency

Goroutines

Goroutines are lightweight threads.

```go
go func() {
    fmt.Println("Hello from Goroutine")
}()
```

Channels

Channels are used for communication between goroutines.

```go
ch := make(chan int)
```

```go
go func() {

    ch <- 42 // Send value

}()



fmt.Println(<-ch) // Receive value: 42
```

---

9. Error Handling

Errors in Go are values.

go

```go
func divide(a, b int) (int, error) {

    if b == 0 {

        return  0,  fmt.Errorf("division  by
zero")

    }

    return a / b, nil
```

```go
}

result, err := divide(10, 0)

if err != nil {

    fmt.Println("Error:", err)

} else {

    fmt.Println("Result:", result)

}
```

---

10. File I/O

Reading a File

go

```go
data, err := os.ReadFile("file.txt")

if err != nil {

    log.Fatal(err)

}

fmt.Println(string(data))
```

Writing to a File

go

```go
err := os.WriteFile("file.txt",
[]byte("Hello, Go!"), 0644)

if err != nil {

    log.Fatal(err)

}
```

---

11. Testing

Go has a built-in testing framework.

go

```go
package main

import "testing"

func TestAdd(t *testing.T) {

    result := add(2, 3)

    if result != 5 {

        t.Errorf("Expected 5, got %d",
result)
```

```go
    }
}
```

Run tests using:

bash

```bash
go test
```

Practical Exercise

Task: Create a Simple Calculator

1. Write a program that performs basic arithmetic operations.
2. Use functions for each operation.
3. Allow user input for numbers and operations.

Solution:

go

```go
package main

import (

    "fmt"

)


func add(a, b float64) float64 {
```

```go
        return a + b
    }


    func subtract(a, b float64) float64 {
        return a - b
    }


    func main() {
        var a, b float64
        var op string

        fmt.Println("Enter first number:")
        fmt.Scan(&a)
        fmt.Println("Enter an operator (+ or -
    ):")
        fmt.Scan(&op)
        fmt.Println("Enter second number:")
        fmt.Scan(&b)
```

```go
switch op {

case "+":

    fmt.Println("Result:", add(a, b))

case "-":

    fmt.Println("Result",    subtract(a,
b))

    default:

    fmt.Println("Invalid operator")

    }

}
```

Appendix B: Tools and Libraries for Web Development with Go

Web development with Go is made efficient and scalable by leveraging a rich ecosystem of tools and libraries. This appendix introduces you to the most widely used tools and libraries for building web applications, managing dependencies, and enhancing productivity. Each tool or library is explained in detail, with examples and practical applications to ensure you can integrate them seamlessly into your projects.

---

1. Web Frameworks

1.1 Gin

Gin is a fast, lightweight web framework ideal for building RESTful APIs and web applications.

Key Features:

- Fast performance due to its zero-memory allocation.
- Built-in middleware for routing, logging, and error handling.

Example:

go

```go
package main

import (

    "github.com/gin-gonic/gin"

)

func main() {

    r := gin.Default()

    // Define a GET endpoint
```

```go
    r.GET("/ping", func(c *gin.Context) {

        c.JSON(200, gin.H{

            "message": "pong",

        })

    })

    // Start the server

    r.Run() // Default port: 8080

}
```

Use Case: Gin is perfect for creating lightweight and high-performance APIs.

1.2 Echo

Echo is another minimalist web framework with a focus on simplicity and performance.

Key Features:

- High extensibility with middleware support.
- Built-in template rendering.

Example:

go

```go
package main

import (

    "net/http"

    "github.com/labstack/echo/v4"

)


func main() {

    e := echo.New()


    // Define a route

    e.GET("/", func(c echo.Context) error {

        return        c.String(http.StatusOK,
"Hello, Echo!")

    })


    // Start the server

    e.Start(":8080")
```

```
}
```

Use Case: Echo is ideal for applications requiring robust middleware and templating support.

---

2. Database Libraries

2.1 GORM

GORM is a powerful ORM library for Go that simplifies database interactions.

Key Features:

- Supports multiple databases (MySQL, PostgreSQL, SQLite, etc.).
- Automatic table migrations.

Example:

go

```go
package main

import (

    "gorm.io/driver/sqlite"

    "gorm.io/gorm"
```

```go
)

type User struct {

    ID    uint    `gorm:"primaryKey"`

    Name string

    Age    int

}

func main() {

    db,                 err              :=
gorm.Open(sqlite.Open("test.db"),
&gorm.Config{})

    if err != nil {

        panic("failed to connect database")

    }

    // Migrate the schema

    db.AutoMigrate(&User{})

    // Create a user

    db.Create(&User{Name: "John", Age: 25})

}
```

Use Case: GORM is suitable for projects requiring advanced ORM features.

2.2 sqlx

sqlx is an extension of Go's `database/sql` package with additional functionality.

Key Features:

- Simplifies working with raw SQL queries.
- Supports struct scanning.

Example:

```go
package main

import (

    "database/sql"

    "fmt"

    "github.com/jmoiron/sqlx"

    _ "github.com/mattn/go-sqlite3"

)
```

```go
type User struct {
    ID   int    `db:"id"`
    Name string `db:"name"`
    Age  int    `db:"age"`
}


func main() {
    db, err := sqlx.Open("sqlite3",
"test.db")
    if err != nil {
        panic(err)
    }
    // Query users
    var users []User
    db.Select(&users, "SELECT * FROM users")
    fmt.Println(users)
}
```

Use Case: sqlx is ideal for developers who prefer working directly with SQL.

---

3. Authentication Libraries

3.1 Authboss

Authboss is a modular authentication library for Go.

Key Features:

- Provides user authentication, registration, and password recovery.
- Supports OAuth2 integration.

Example: Refer to the Authboss documentation for detailed usage.

Use Case: Use Authboss for projects requiring comprehensive user authentication.

3.2 JWT (github.com/dgrijalva/jwt-go)

JWT is a popular library for implementing JSON Web Tokens.

Example:

go

```go
package main

import (

    "fmt"

    "github.com/dgrijalva/jwt-go"

    "time"

)

func main() {

    token                          :=
jwt.NewWithClaims(jwt.SigningMethodHS256,
jwt.MapClaims{

        "username": "user1",

        "exp":        time.Now().Add(time.Hour
* 1).Unix(),

    })

    tokenString,            err              :=
token.SignedString([]byte("secret"))

    if err != nil {

        panic(err)

    }
```

```go
    fmt.Println("Token:", tokenString)
}
```

Use Case: JWT is ideal for stateless authentication in APIs.

---

4. Utility Libraries

4.1 Viper

Viper is a configuration management library.

Example:

```go
go
package main

import (

    "fmt"

    "github.com/spf13/viper"

)


func main() {

    viper.SetConfigName("config")
```

```go
    viper.SetConfigType("json")

    viper.AddConfigPath(".")


    err := viper.ReadInConfig()

    if err != nil {

        panic(err)

    }



    fmt.Println("Database                    Host:",
viper.GetString("database.host"))

}
```

Use Case: Viper is perfect for managing configuration files in various formats.

4.2 Logrus

Logrus is a structured logging library.

Example:

go

```go
package main

import (

    log "github.com/sirupsen/logrus"

)

func main() {

    log.WithFields(log.Fields{

        "username": "user1",

    }).Info("User logged in")

}
```

Use Case: Logrus is ideal for adding structured logging to your application.

---

5. Deployment and Monitoring Tools

5.1 Docker

Docker simplifies application deployment by containerizing your application.

Use Case: Refer to the Docker chapter for detailed usage.

5.2 Prometheus and Grafana

Prometheus is used for metrics collection, and Grafana visualizes the data.

Use Case: Integrate Prometheus and Grafana for monitoring your web application.

Practical Exercise

Task: Build a REST API with Gin and GORM

1. Set up a Gin-based web server.
2. Use GORM to interact with a SQLite database.
3. Implement CRUD operations.

Solution:

go

```go
// Complete example combining Gin and GORM

package main

import (

    "github.com/gin-gonic/gin"
```

```go
    "gorm.io/driver/sqlite"

    "gorm.io/gorm"

)

type Task struct {

    ID   uint  `json:"id" gorm:"primaryKey"`

    Name string `json:"name"`

}

func main() {

    db,                            _                    :=
gorm.Open(sqlite.Open("test.db"),
&gorm.Config{})

    db.AutoMigrate(&Task{})


    r := gin.Default()


    r.GET("/tasks", func(c *gin.Context) {

        var tasks []Task

        db.Find(&tasks)
```

```go
        c.JSON(200, tasks)

    })


    r.POST("/tasks", func(c *gin.Context) {

        var task Task

        if err := c.ShouldBindJSON(&task);
err == nil {

            db.Create(&task)

            c.JSON(200, task)

        }

    })


    r.Run()

}
```

Appendix C: Debugging and Troubleshooting Common Issues

Debugging and troubleshooting are essential skills for every developer. This appendix provides a comprehensive guide to identifying, diagnosing, and resolving common issues encountered during Go web development. By following these strategies and examples, you will be better equipped to handle errors efficiently and keep your applications running smoothly.

1. Debugging Techniques

1.1 Using `fmt` for Debugging

The simplest way to debug is by printing values using `fmt`.

Example:

```go
package main

import "fmt"

func main() {
    value := 42
```

```go
    fmt.Println("Debugging value:", value) //
Prints: Debugging value: 42

}
```

Tip: Use descriptive messages to make logs easier to understand.

1.2 Using the `log` Package

The `log` package is a step up from `fmt` for debugging and logging.

Example:

```go
go
package main

import "log"

func main() {

    log.Println("Starting application...")

    log.Println("Performing operation...")

    log.Fatal("Encountered       a        critical
error!") // Terminates the program

}
```

Use Case: Use `log` for structured debugging and to identify critical issues.

1.3 Using Debugging Tools

- **Delve (dlv)**: A powerful debugger for Go applications.
  - Install Delve: `go install github.com/go-delve/delve/cmd/dlv@latest`
  - Start debugging: `dlv debug main.go`
  - Use breakpoints, step through code, and inspect variables.

Example:

sh

```
dlv debug main.go

(dlv) break main.go:10

(dlv) continue

(dlv) print value
```

Tip: Delve is invaluable for debugging complex issues in real-time.

---

2. Common Errors and Solutions

2.1 Compilation Errors

Compilation errors occur when the Go compiler detects invalid syntax or types.

Example:

go

```
package main

func main() {

    x := "42"

    y := x + 1 // Error: mismatched types string and int

}
```

Solution:

- Check error messages for line numbers and details.

Fix type mismatches:

go

```
package main

import "strconv"
```

```go
func main() {

    x := "42"

    y, _ := strconv.Atoi(x) // Convert string
to int

    z := y + 1

    fmt.Println(z)

}
```

2.2 Runtime Errors

Runtime errors occur while the program is running.

Example: Dereferencing a `nil` pointer.

go

```go
package main

func main() {

    var ptr *int

    *ptr = 42 // Panic: runtime error: invalid
memory address

}
```

Solution:

Check for `nil` values before dereferencing:
go

```go
if ptr != nil {
    *ptr = 42
} else {
    fmt.Println("Pointer is nil")
}
```

2.3 Logical Errors

Logical errors produce incorrect results without crashing the program.

Example:

go

```go
package main

func main() {
    sum := 0

    for i := 1; i <= 10; i++ {
```

```
        sum -= i // Should be sum += i

    }

    fmt.Println("Sum:", sum)

}
```

Solution:

- Use print statements or a debugger to trace variable values.
- Write unit tests to validate logic.

---

3. Debugging Web Applications

3.1 HTTP Handlers Not Working

Check if the correct route is defined.

Example:

go

```
package main

import (

    "net/http"

)
```

```go
func main() {

    http.HandleFunc("/hello",          func(w
http.ResponseWriter, r *http.Request) {

        w.Write([]byte("Hello, World!"))

    })

    http.ListenAndServe(":8080", nil)

}
```

Common Issues:

- Incorrect URL path.
- Missing trailing slashes.

Solution: Ensure the route matches exactly and use a logging middleware to trace requests.

3.2 Database Connection Errors

Example:

go

```go
package main

import (
```

```go
    "database/sql"

    _ "github.com/lib/pq"
)

func main() {

    db, err := sql.Open("postgres",
"user=wrong password=wrong dbname=test
sslmode=disable")

    if err != nil {

        panic(err) // Outputs: invalid
connection parameters

    }

    defer db.Close()

}
```

Solution:

- Verify connection strings.

Use ping to test the connection:
go
```go
if err := db.Ping(); err != nil {
```

```go
    log.Fatal("Database connection failed:",
err)

}
```

---

4. Best Practices for Debugging

1. **Log Everything**:
   - Use structured logging libraries like Logrus or Zap.

Example:
go

```go
log.WithFields(log.Fields{

    "module": "main",

    "status": "running",

}).Info("Application started")
```

   -

2. **Test Early and Often**:
   - Write unit tests for each function.

Use `go` `test` to `run` tests:
sh
```sh
go test ./...
```

3. **Monitor Application Metrics**:
   - ○ Use Prometheus and Grafana for real-time monitoring.
   - ○ Track request latencies, error rates, and system health.
4. **Set Up Alerts**:
   - ○ Configure alerts for critical metrics like high error rates or CPU usage.

---

5. Practical Exercise

Task: Debug a Web Application with Errors

Scenario: A simple web server has multiple issues. Fix them.

Code:

```go
package main

import (

    "fmt"

    "net/http"

)

func main() {
```

```go
http.HandleFunc("/hello",                func(w
http.ResponseWriter, r *http.Request) {

        name := r.URL.Query().Get("name")

        if name == "" {

                fmt.Fprint(w, "Hello, Guest!") //
Missing return

        }

        fmt.Fprintf(w, "Hello, %s!", name)

    })

    err := http.ListenAndServe(":8080", nil)

    if err != nil {

        fmt.Println("Server error:", err) //
Should use log.Fatal

    }

}
```

Steps:

1. **Identify the Issue:**
   - Missing `return` causes the second `fmt.Fprintf` to execute.

Fix the Code:

go

```go
if name == "" {

    fmt.Fprint(w, "Hello, Guest!")

    return

}
```

2. **Enhance Logging:** Replace `fmt.Println` with `log.Fatal`.

3. **Test:**
   ○ Run the server and test with different query parameters.

---

www.ingramcontent.com/pod-product-compliance
Lightning Source LLC
Chambersburg PA
CBHW082106070326
40689CB00055B/4765